Vedic As

Applications of
Yogini Dasha
for Brilliant Predictions

Rajeev Jhanji

N K Sharma

Edited by **Dr. K S Charak**

UMA
PUBLICATIONS

Applications of
Yogini Dasha
for Brilliant Predictions

© Rajeev Jhanji

Email: rajeev@jhanji.com

First Edition   : June 1994
Second Edition : May 1998
Third Edition   : May 2018

ISBN 978-93-81769-02-7

Price:
US$19.95

Cover:
VAJRAYOGINI (Buddhist Deity). Tibet, 1400-1499, Copper.

Published by:
UMA PUBLICATIONS
72 Gagan Vihar, New Delhi - 110051, INDIA.

Printed by:
CreateSpace, An Amazon.com Company

PREFACE TO THE THIRD EDITION

Publication of the *Applications of Yogini Dasha* for the first time in the year 1994 introduced to the lover of Vedic astrology a long used and highly reliable dasha system which had gone into virtual oblivion except in some of the northern hilly states of India. This dasha system has been used by its proponents in addition to or as an effective alternative to the well-known Vimshottari dasha. This work was the result of a serious research by Rajeev Jhanji and N K Sharma who those days used to teach at the astrology school of the Bharatiya Vidya Bhavan in New Delhi (India). The second edition of this book came in the year 1998 and was soon exhausted. After that the book remained unavailable for nearly two decades though its demand never really waned. The main reason for the unavailability of this precious work was that one of the authors, Rajeev Jhanji, moved out of India to USA in the year 1999 while the other, N K Sharma, prematurely left this world for the heavenly abode. Relentless demand for this book both by the student as well as the savant of astrology prompted us to bring out the present edition of this valuable work.

This third edition of the *Applications of Yogini Dasha* has been completely revised and enlarged. A lot of additional astrological material has been added almost in every chapter. Some new example charts have been included in this edition while birth details of several important individuals discussed in this book have been provided for the benefit of the student. We hope that the reader would find this enlarged and enriched edition of one of the most reliable and accurate dasha systems of Parashara an invaluable tool for predictive brilliance.

April 14, 2018   Dr K S Charak

iv

PREFACE TO THE
FIRST EDITION

This is the first ever book on Yogini dasha not merely in English but, as far as I know, in any language of India. The books available on dasha-systems in India generally deal only with the Vimshottari dasha and give some principles of interpretation without illustrations. Naturally when it came to planning a book on Yogini dasha, we had decided that it had to be a book with profuse illustrations.

I have had no prejudice against Yogini dasha unlike some well-known astrologers of India who reject it because it has a very short cycle of thirty-six years only. The ticklish question was how to apply this dasha in the cases of those who had crossed the age of thirty-six and were less than seventy-two years when two cycles of Yogini dasha would be over. The more ticklish problem was how to use this for persons above the age of seventy-two years when the third cycle of Yogini dasha would be in operation.

My problem was solved accidentally when during my career as a government officer, I heard that a peon (the lowest rung in official hierarchy) had predicted to someone in the office about impending danger to his health which did happen. I called the peon, who was from Garhwal, a Himalayan state in northern India, and asked how he had made that prediction? He told me that he first used Yogini dasha and then combined the Vimshottari dasha. Then he told me that he progressed the Yogini dasha according to the age of the man concerned and gave me some future predictions which came out correct. *How he did this progression he never explained to me.* He wanted to keep it as a family secret, which he had been instructed by his father, also his guru, not to disclose it to anyone.

I was convinced that Yogini dasha worked in all cases whatever be the age of the native, if it was combined with the Vimshottari dasha. But I do not know how Yogini is progressed yet I found amazingly correct results by adopting his approach. The peon impressed me more because he came to the right prediction with amazing speed. Rajeev Jhanji and N.K. Sharma started their intensive work on Yogini dasha after their Visharad and even gave very good predictions on the lines and method which my office peon had told me about.

I am happy to present this book before the astrological audiences with the assurance that Yogini dasha, if used intelligently, would work with amazing accuracy, even if there is some error in anyone's birth-time but the ascendant is correct. In Yogini some error in the degree of the Moon is tolerable as the error in timing an event will go wrong by some weeks only.

The most attractive features of this book are:

(a) It has been shown how with the help of Yogini dasha dependable predictions can be given.

(b) How when combined with the Vimshottari dasha, the results obtained are more dependable.

(c) When divisional horoscopes too are used, results are spectacular.

(d) When both the Yogini and Vimshottari dasha are used both on the birth horoscope and divisional horoscopes, a pin-pointed timing along with the nature of psychology operating, resulting into an action and getting expressed as an event, can be done with immense confidence.

(e) Some very significant and classical hints on how the karakas (significators) like, the Sun for the father and the Moon for the mother, along with the relevant houses like, the fourth for mother, the third for brother, etc., are used and demonstrated in the book.

In that sense, it is a book not merely on Yogini dasha but transcending that narrow orbit, shows how techniques of Vedic astrology can be employed to interpret divisional horoscopes. In the significant march of astrological renaissance of our decades, this book is bound to become a very significant landmark.

May 21, 1994   K N Rao

ABOUT THE AUTHORS

Rajeev Jhanji *B.Com., Diploma in Printing Technology, Diploma (Hons.) in Systems Management, Jyotish Visharad*

Rajeev Jhanji is an eminent scholar and teacher of Vedic astrology. He has taught astrology for several years to hundreds of students in the Institute of Astrology of the Bharatiya Vidya Bhavan, New Delhi. By profession a computer expert, a printer and a publisher, he has a profound understanding of the astronomical/mathematical part of astrology of which he is an authority. His beautiful graphic depiction of the zodiac and its astrological elements, serialised in the pages of the bi-monthly *Vedic Astrology* of which he has been the Associate Editor, has earned him wide acclaim.

Rajeev is equally well versed in both the Parashari as well as the Jaimini systems of astrology which he employs simultaneously with great success. Research into the operation of the dasha systems is his area of specialisation and the present work, *Applications of Yogini Dasha*, has been a consequence of this interest of his. Incidentally, this happens to be the first authentic work on the method of application of the Yogini dasha. Rajeev has an uncanny insight into the subtle principles of mundane and electional astrology as well as natal horoscopy. His departure to USA in the year 1999 has been a loss to his Indian students.

N K Sharma *B.Sc., B.Ed., Jyotish Visharad*

N K Sharma was an honorary teacher at the Institute of Astrology of the Bharatiya Vidya Bhavan, New Delhi. With his scientific background, he had an impressive and lucid style of teaching which made him a highly sought-after teacher of astrology among his students. He had a keen interest in experimenting with the varied principles of astrology and testing them on actual horoscopic charts to determine their extent of authenticity and their limitations.

Sharma, like Rajeev, was a keen advocate of using multiple dasha schemes to a given horoscope. Had destiny not cut short his life, he would have contributed immensely to astrological knowledge. Born on April 27, 1967, he left us prematurely on May 19, 1999, an irreparable loss to his friends, colleagues and the astrological world.

CONTENTS

S E C T I O N   I

S E C T I O N   I I

S E C T I O N   I I I

CHAPTER ONE

INTRODUCTION:
WHY YOGINI DASHA

This is the first ever book on the use of Yogini dasha for successful predictions with profuse illustrations. It is well known that eighty percent of successful predictive techniques of Vedic astrology are lost or hidden in the *parampara* (tradition) and only twenty percent are given in the available classical works. Even in these classical works the results ascribed to them have been put in such a veiled way as to clarify less and confuse more. For instance, Sankata (Rahu) literally means trouble. But just as a well-placed Rahu in Vimshottari dasha can give extraordinary results,* so also Sankata dasha can be productive of extra-ordinarily good results. Therefore, the Sanskrit terminology used must be interpreted liberally not literally, flexibly not dogmatically, and conjointly not severally.

This book was originally conceived as a research paper which Mr. K.N. Rao wanted to present during a day-long course on November 23, 1993 at the Second International Symposium of the American Council of Vedic Astrology at San Francisco. During the production of this paper, the following points received special consideration:

(a) The role of the Yogini dasha as an independent tool for the timing of events.

---

* See Kennedy's Rahu in fourth house, p.149.

2

(b) The use of the Yogini dasha along with the Vimshottari for a double check of the timing of an event.

(c) Could the Yogini dasha, in spite of being a dasha of only thirty six years, be applied all through one's life by repeating the thirty six year cycle? We illustrated this by taking three examples: the first of Sanjay Gandhi (the second son of late prime minister of India, Indira Gandhi), 1946-1980, who died in the first cycle; John F Kennedy of USA (1917-1963) who died in the second cycle; and Pandit Jawaharlal Nehru, the first prime minister of India (1889-1964), who died in the third cycle.

(d) Ever since we learnt the Yogini dasha, we have been using it effectively for our day-to-day predictions very successfully. Our friend Dr. K.S. Charak has been so fascinated by the Yogini dasha that in his book, *Essentials of Medical Astrology*, he has presented his astro-medical case studies by employing both the Vimshottari and the Yogini dashas.

(e) The Yogini dasha is the finest, shortest and the most effective tool for precise predictions in a well-defined time frame.

(f) The greatest advantage of using the Yogini dasha is that some errors in calculation of the degree of the Moon do not affect the predictable results significantly. In the case of Kaala Chakra dasha, for example, an error of one minute in the degree of the Moon can make a difference of six months in a 100 year cycle and an error of 10 minutes can result in a staggering error of 5 years. In the case of Yogini dasha, on the other hand, a mistake even of 20 minutes can make a difference of very few months only, in the dasha of Sankata (8 years) and of a few days only in the dasha of Mangala (1 year).

It must be for this reason that all experienced astrologers of northern India, particularly in the Himalayan states of Jammu and Kashmir, Himachal Pradesh, Kumaon and Gharwal, refuse to give predictions unless the Yogini dasha is calculated first.

Like Jaimini's Chara dasha, the Yogini dasha can be calculated mentally on a given horoscope within a few minutes even while walking on a road. There is no reason why such a successful and effective dasha should not be employed more widely by Vedic astrologers all over the world.

This is a product of our research on hundreds of horoscopes done initially at micro level and later at macro level. We started initially with four or five horoscopes to make an in-depth analysis; when we got accurate results, we increased the number of horoscopes to hundreds. Later, we extended this to make a broader study by bringing into use related divisional horoscopes or the vargas also.

The principles followed uniformly in this book are:

(a) Using the Yogini dasha along with the Vimshottari.

(b) Interpreting the dasha both from the lagna and the Moon.

(c) Interpreting the dasha both from the lagna and from the concerned *Karaka* or significator, for instance the Sun for father, the Moon for mother, etc.

All that we have endeavoured to do in this book is to throw into different permutations and combinations various classical principles given in standard astrological texts like the *Brihat Parashara Hora Shastra*, the *Mansagari*, the *Brihat Jataka*, the *Saravali*, etc.

But this book is essentially a product of our fundamental research in the use of the Yogini dasha which is the best astrological mirror for explaining at a glance the current problem of an individual.

Let it be illustrated here. Given below is the horo-scope of the erstwhile President Bill Clinton of the USA. We have taken his birth particulars as August 19, 1946; 8:51 hours; at Hope, Arkansas, USA. That gives him Kanya (Virgo) lagna at 12°23'. Now let us apply the Yogini dasha on the events of Clinton's life.

	Moon 27°11'	Rahu	
	Bill Clinton 19 August 1944 8:51 am Hope, Arkansas	Saturn Mercury	
		Sun	
	Ketu	Jupiter	Lagna Venus Mars

Jupiter 7	Lagna Venus Mars	Sun 5	4 Saturn Mercury
Ketu 8			
10 11	9 3 12 6		2 Rahu
		1 Moon 27°11'	

Lagna	12°23'	Mars	13°12'	Venus	17°54'
Sun	2°45'	Mercury	14°20'	Saturn	9°00'
Moon	27°11'	Jupiter	0°06'	Rahu	25°09'

Marriage

When he got married in October 1975, he was running the dasha of Bhramari-Siddha (Mars-Venus). Mars is with Venus in the lagna and both are aspecting his seventh house of marriage. Venus is also the Karaka for marriage, associ-ated with Mars. Both Mars and Venus aspect the seventh house from the Karaka for marriage, Venus. The dasha of Mars-Venus is eminently suited for marriage.

Birth of Daughter

After a gap of over four years when his daughter was born on February 27, 1980, he was passing through the dasha of Bhadrika-Sankata (Mercury-Rahu). Mercury is associated with Saturn, the fifth lord of children, and as-pects the fifth house. Rahu occupies the ninth house, the alternate house for progeny, the fifth from the fifth. Rahu also gives results according to its dispositor (the lord of the house where planet is placed) which, in this case, is Venus in the lagna aspected by the fifth lord Saturn.

US Presidentship

Billl Clinton was sworn in as the US President on January 20, 1993. He was running the dasha of Siddha-Bhramari (Venus-Mars). The seeds for his election were sown in the earlier dasha of Siddha-Dhanya (Venus-Jupiter) which period coincided with the election campaign and which created a wave of popularity in his favour. Siddha (Venus) is the dasha of the ninth house of good fortune. Jupiter (Dhanya) is the lord of the seventh house of position and status, and aspects the tenth house. Mars (Bhramari) sub-period that followed has the beneficence derived from the association of Mars with the ninth lord. It would be appreciated eventually that Mars-Venus combination ensures a high status blemished with controversies and humiliating situations.

Controversies

Siddha (Venus) dasha (May 1988 to May 1995) got him involved in controversies. Venus, although the highly favourable ninth lord, is under heavy affliction. It associates with the eighth lord (disgrace) Mars in the lagna. It is debilitated and also aspected by the sixth lord (enmity) Saturn. These afflictions drag him in the controversial land deals and sex scandals relating to his tenure as the Governor of the state of Arkansas. *From the Moon*, Venus (Siddha) is the lord of second and seventh houses (double killer), placed in the sixth house with the eighth lord, Mars.

Mercury (Bhadrika) is the tenth lord placed with Saturn, the sixth lord of court cases. *From the Moon*, Mercury is the sixth lord associated with the tenth lord, Saturn. Siddha-Bhadrika (Venus-Mercury), and subsequently Siddha-Ulka (Venus-Saturn), dragged him into legal issues in the USA.

US President Second Term

It was in Sankata-Sankata (Rahu-Rahu) that he was re-elected as the President of the USA, and sworn in on January 20, 1997. Exalted Rahu occupies the ninth house of the rashi chart. As Rahu represents it dispositor Venus, this term too was embroiled in controversies. On August 17, 1998, he admitted to sexual relationship with Lewinsky, with loss of face and with impeachment proceedings against him starting from December 19, 1998. He was running

Summary of the Events

Event	Yogini Dasha	Relationship
Marriage Oct. 1975	Bhramari-Siddha (Mars-Venus)	Mars and Venus in lagna aspect 7th house
Daughter born Feb. 27, 1980	Badrika-Sankata (Mercury-Rahu)	Mercury with 5th lord, aspects 5th house. Rahu's dispositor Venus aspected by 5th lord
Presidential campaign 1992	Siddha-Dhanya (Venus-Jupiter)	9th lord Venus in lagna 7th lord Jupiter aspects the 10th house
US President Jan. 20, 1993	Siddha-Bhramari (Venus-Mars)	Mars with 9th lord. Ven+Mar = high status, controversy, humilation
Legal Issues 1993-95	Siddha-Bhadrika (Venus-Mercury) Siddha-Ulka (Venus-Saturn)	Venus deb.; with 8 lord Mars; aspect of 6 lord. -Mercury: 10L with 6L -Saturn: 6L with 10L
US President 2nd term Jan. 20, 1997	Sankata-Sankata (Rahu-Rahu)	Rahu exalted in 9th house.
Sex scandal (Aug. 1998) Impeachment Dec. 19, 1998	Sankata-Bhramari (Rahu-Mars)	Rahu: dispositor Venus debilitated & afflicted by 8th lord Mars.
Wife contested Presidential election Nov. 8, 2016	Bhadrika-Sankata (Mercury-Rahu)	For spouse, treat 7H as lagna: Mer. with Sat. Rahu's dispositor Venus deb. in 7H, with Mars.

Sankata-Bhramari (Rahu-Mars) at that time. Both Rahu and Mars have sufficient affliction to justify the events. The same dasha saw him acquitted. Jupiter's aspect on the tenth house is the saving grace.

Wife Contested Presidential Election

Hillary Clinton, his wife, contested the US Presidential election in the year 2016. She conceded defeat to Donald Trump on November 8, 2016. Bill Clinton was running the dasha of Bhadrika-Sankata (Mercury-Rahu) at that time. Mercury, his lagna lord, is the lord of the seventh house (spouse) *from the seventh* (to be considered as the lagna of the spouse) associated with Saturn. Rahu is placed in the eighth house *from his seventh lord* Jupiter (which itself is placed in the eighth *from the seventh house*). Rahu also represents its dispositor Venus which is debilitated in the seventh house *from his seventh* (i.e., in his lagna) and happens to be the debilitated eighth lord in the seventh, *from the seventh house*, the lagna of the spouse. Elsewhere we have mentioned that the dasha of the second lord may prove difficult for the spouse.

Conclusion

Here we have given in this introduction only an illustrative example to show how through the Yogini dasha significant life events can be gleaned using a birth horoscope alone. Much clearer results would become obvious when we use the vargas or divisional charts. While the Yogini dasha can be employed alone in chart analysis, as in the above example, the results would improve remarkably when we use the Vimshottari dasha in addition.

In conclusion, it must be stated that while a spiritual person can afford to make a tryst with eternity, modern man has to care for the fleeting moments of his life. Can there be any dasha superior to the Yogini in understanding the joys and sorrows of those fleeting moments better?

CHAPTER TWO

CALCULATION OF YOGINI DASHA

According to *Brihat Parashara Hora Shastra*, Yogini dasha was revealed by Lord Shiva to Goddess Parvati. There are eight types of Yoginis. The order in which these eight Yoginis operate, their lords and dasha periods are given in table II-1. After the end of a cycle, the next cycle starts again with Mangala.

Table II-1
Order of Yoginis, their lords and dasha periods

S.No.	Yogini	Lord	Period
1.	Mangala	Moon	1 year
2.	Pingala	Sun	2 years
3.	Dhanya	Jupiter	3 years
4.	Bhramari	Mars	4 years
5.	Bhadrika	Mercury	5 years
6.	Ulka	Saturn	6 years
7.	Siddha	Venus	7 years
8.	Sankata	Rahu	8 years
		Total Period	36 years

According to classical texts, the planets – the Moon, the Sun, Jupiter, Mars, Mercury, Saturn, Venus, Rahu have been evolved respectively from the Mangala, Pingala, etc.

Like Vimshottari dasha, the Yogini dasha is also a *nakshatrika* dasha based on the constellation of the

Moon, commonly referred to as Rashi nakshatra or janma nakshatra.

In the major period of each Yogini, sub-periods of all Yoginis operate according to their proportional periods in the natural order starting from its own sub period.

Calculation of Yogini Dasha (Traditional Method)

Note down the nakshatra number of the Moon, taking Ashwini as nakshatra number 1. Add three to it. Divide by eight. The remainder represents the Yogini dasha operative at the time of birth.

$$\text{Yogini Dasha at Birth} = \frac{\text{Nak. No. of the Moon} + 3}{8}$$

Remainder	Dasha
1	Mangala
2	Pingala
3	Dhanya
4	Bhramari
5	Bhadrika
6	Ulka
7	Siddha
8 or 0	Sankata

Table II-2 lists the nakshatras and their extents.

Example

A native is born with his Moon in Sagittarius 16°40'. The nakshatra of the Moon is Poorvashadha (nakshatra number 20). So according to the above formula:

$$= \frac{20 + 3}{8} = \frac{23}{8} = \text{Quo: 2; Remainder: 7 (Siddha)}.$$

The balance of dasha is dependent on the degrees remaining to be traversed by the Moon in its nakshatra.

Table II-2
Nakshatras and their extents

No. Nakshatra	Extent from	to	*Yogini*	Vimshottari lord yrs	lord yrs
1. Ashwini	0ˢ00°00'	0ˢ13°20'	Bhramari	Mars 4	Ketu 7
2. Bharani	0ˢ13°20'	0ˢ26°40'	Bhadrika	Mer 5	Ven 20
3. Krittika	0ˢ26°40'	1ˢ10°00'	Ulka	Saturn 6	Sun 6
4. Rohini	1ˢ10°00'	1ˢ23°20'	Siddha	Venus 7	Mon 10
5. Mrigashira	1ˢ23°20'	2ˢ06°40'	Sankata	Rahu 8	Mars 7
6. Ardra	2ˢ06°40'	2ˢ20°00'	Mangala	Moon 1	Rahu 18
7. Punarvasu	2ˢ20°00'	3ˢ03°20'	Pingala	Sun 2	Jup 16
8. Pushya	3ˢ03°20'	3ˢ16°40'	Dhanya	Jupiter 3	Sat 19
9. Ashlesha	3ˢ16°40'	4ˢ00°00'	Bhramari	Mars 4	Mer 17
10 Magha	4ˢ00°00'	4ˢ13°20'	Bhadrika	Mer 5	Ketu 7
11. Poorva Phalguni	4ˢ13°20'	4ˢ26°40'	Ulka	Saturn 6	Ven 20
12. Uttara Phalguni	4ˢ26°40'	5ˢ10°00'	Siddha	Venus 7	Sun 6
13. Hasta	5ˢ10°00'	5ˢ23°20'	Sankata	Rahu 8	Mon 10
14. Chitra	5ˢ23°20'	6ˢ06°40'	Mangala	Moon 1	Mars 7
15. Swati	6ˢ06°40'	6ˢ20°00'	Pingala	Sun 2	Rahu 18
16. Vishakha	6ˢ20°00'	7ˢ03°20'	Dhanya	Jupiter 3	Jup 16
17. Anuradha	7ˢ03°20'	7ˢ16°40'	Bhramari	Mars 4	Sat 19
18. Jyeshtha	7ˢ16°40'	8ˢ00°00'	Bhadrika	Mer 5	Mer 17
19. Moola	8ˢ00°00'	8ˢ13°20'	Ulka	Saturn 6	Ketu 7
20. Poorvashadha	8ˢ13°20'	8ˢ26°40'	Siddha	Venus 7	Ven 20
21. Uttarashadha	8ˢ26°40'	9ˢ10°00'	Sankata	Rahu 8	Sun 6
22. Sravana	9ˢ10°00'	9ˢ23°20'	Mangala	Moon 1	Mon 10
23. Dhanishtha	9ˢ23°20'	10ˢ06°40'	Pingala	Sun 2	Mars 7
24. Shatabhishaj	10ˢ06°40'	10ˢ20°00'	Dhanya	Jupiter 3	Rahu 18
25. Poorva Bhadrapada	10ˢ20°00'	11ˢ03°20'	Bhramari	Mars 4	Jup 16
26. Uttara Bhadrapada	11ˢ03°20'	11ˢ16°40'	Bhadrika	Mer 5	Sat 19
27. Revati	11ˢ16°40'	12ˢ00°00'	Ulka	Saturn 6	Mer 17

Calculate the balance of degrees to be covered by the Moon in its nakshatra. Multiply by the period of dasha operative at the time of birth. Divide by full span of a nakshatra (13°20'). The result represents the balance of the Yogini dasha operative at the time of birth.

$$\text{Yogini Dasha Balance} = \frac{\substack{\text{Period of} \\ \text{Yogini Dasha}} \times \substack{\text{Balance of degrees yet} \\ \text{to be covered by the} \\ \text{Moon in its nakshatra}}}{13°20'}$$

In the above example, the Moon's longitude is $8^{s}16°40'$ and the extent of Poorvashadha nakshatra is from $8^{s}13°20'$ to $8^{s}26°40'$. The balance of degrees to be covered by the Moon in Poorvashadha nakshatra = $8^{s}26°40' - 8^{s}16°40' = 10°0'$.

The dasha operative was Siddha (period 7 years).

According to the formula, the balance of Siddha Dasha =

$$= \frac{7 \text{ years} \times 10°0'}{13°20'}$$

= 5 years - 3 months - 0 days.

Calculation of Yogini Dasha (Modern Method)

The above method is simplified by adopting the following four steps:

Step 1

Note down the longitude of the Moon. Table II-3 lists the dasha operative at the time of birth from the longitude of the Moon.

Step 2

Refer to the relevant dasha in Table II-4 and find out the balance of dasha from the nearest lower figure to the longitude of the Moon. The table is at an interval of 40 minutes.

Table II-3
Yogini Dasha by Longitude of the Moon

Long. of Moon	Sign	Yogini	Dasha Lord	Sign	Yogini	Dasha Lord	Sign	Yogini	Dasha Lord
0°00' – 13°20'	Aries	Bhramari	Mars	Leo	Bhadrika	Mercury	Sagittarius	Ulka	Saturn
13°20' – 26°40'		Bhadrika	Mercury		Ulka	Saturn		Siddha	Venus
26°40' – 30°00'		Ulka	Saturn		Siddha	Venus		Sankata	Rahu
0°00' – 10°00'	Taurus	Ulka	Saturn	Virgo	Siddha	Venus	Capricorn	Sankata	Rahu
10°00' – 23°20'		Siddha	Venus		Sankata	Rahu		Mangala	Moon
23°20' – 30°00'		Sankata	Rahu		Mangala	Moon		Pingala	Sun
0°00' – 6°40'	Gemini	Sankata	Rahu	Libra	Mangala	Moon	Aquarius	Pingala	Sun
6°40' – 20°00'		Mangala	Moon		Pingala	Sun		Dhanya	Jupiter
20°00' – 30°00'		Pingala	Sun		Dhanya	Jupiter		Bhramari	Mars
0°00' – 3°20'	Cancer	Pingala	Sun	Scorpio	Dhanya	Jupiter	Pisces	Bhramari	Mars
3°20' – 16°40'		Dhanya	Jupiter		Bhramari	Mars		Bhadrika	Mercury
16°40' – 30°00'		Bhramari	Mars		Bhadrika	Mercury		Ulka	Saturn

Table II-4 : Balance of Yogini Dasha by Longitude of the Moon

MANGALA

| Longitude of the Moon | | | Mangala |
Ardra Gemini	Chitra Virgo	Sravana Capricorn	(1 year) y-m-d
6°40'	23°20'	10°00'	1-00-00
7°20'	24°00'	10°40'	0-11-12
8°00'	24°40'	11°20'	0-10-24
8°40'	25°20'	12°00'	0-10-06
9°20'	26°00'	12°40'	0-09-18
10°00'	26°40'	13°20'	0-09-00
10°40'	27°20'	14°00'	0-08-12
11°20'	28°00'	14°40'	0-07-24
12°00'	28°40'	15°20'	0-07-06
12°40'	29°20'	16°00'	0-06-18
13°20'	30°00'	16°40'	0-06-00
14°00'	Lib 0°40'	17°20'	0-05-12
14°40'	1°20'	18°00'	0-04-24
15°20'	2°00'	18°40'	0-04-06
16°00'	2°40'	19°20'	0-03-18
16°40'	3°20'	20°00'	0-03-00
17°20'	4°00'	20°40'	0-02-12
18°00'	4°40'	21°20'	0-01-24
18°40'	5°20'	22°00'	0-01-06
19°20'	6°00'	22°40'	0-00-18
20°00'	6°40'	23°20'	0-00-00

PINGALA

| Longitude of the Moon | | | Pingala |
Punarvasu Gemini	Swati Libra	Dhanishtha Capricorn	(2 years) y-m-d
20°00'	6°40'	23°20'	2-00-00
20°40'	7°20'	24°00'	1-10-24
21°20'	8°00'	24°40'	1-09-18
22°00'	8°40'	25°20'	1-08-12
22°40'	9°20'	26°00'	1-07-06
23°20'	10°00'	26°40'	1-06-00
24°00'	10°40'	27°20'	1-04-24
24°40'	11°20'	28°00'	1-03-18
25°20'	12°00'	28°40'	1-02-12
26°00'	12°40'	29°20'	1-01-06
26°40'	13°20'	30°00'	1-00-00
27°20'	14°00'	Aqu 0°40'	0-10-24
28°00'	14°40'	1°20'	0-09-18
28°40'	15°20'	2°00'	0-08-12
29°20'	16°00'	2°40'	0-07-06
30°00'	16°40'	3°20'	0-06-00
Can 0°40'	17°20'	4°00'	0-04-24
1°20'	18°00'	4°40'	0-03-18
2°00'	18°40'	5°20'	0-02-12
2°40'	19°20'	6°00'	0-01-06
3°20'	20°00'	6°40'	0-00-00

14

BHRAMARI

Longitude of Moon				Bhramari (4 years) y-m-d
Ashwini Aries	Ashlesha Cancer	Anuradha Scorpio	P.Bhadrapad Aquarius	
0°00'	16°40'	3°20'	20°00'	4-00-00
0°40'	17°20'	4°00'	20°40'	3-09-18
1°20'	18°00'	4°40'	21°20'	3-07-06
2°00'	18°40'	5°20'	22°00'	3-04-24
2°40'	19°20'	6°00'	22°40'	3-02-12
3°20'	20°00'	6°40'	23°20'	3-00-00
4°00'	20°40'	7°20'	24°00'	2-09-18
4°40'	21°20'	8°00'	24°40'	2-07-06
5°20'	22°00'	8°40'	25°20'	2-04-24
6°00'	22°40'	9°20'	26°00'	2-02-12
6°40'	23°20'	10°00'	26°40'	2-00-00
7°20'	24°00'	10°40'	27°20'	1-09-18
8°00'	24°40'	11°20'	28°00'	1-07-06
8°40'	25°20'	12°00'	28°40'	1-04-24
9°20'	26°00'	12°40'	29°20'	1-02-12
10°00'	26°40'	13°20'	30°00'	1-00-00
10°40'	27°20'	14°00'	Pis 0°40'	0-09-18
11°20'	28°00'	14°40'	1°20'	0-07-06
12°00'	28°40'	15°20'	2°00'	0-04-24
12°40'	29°20'	16°00'	2°40'	0-02-12
13°20'	30°00'	16°40'	3°20'	0-00-00

DHANYA

Longitude of the Moon			Dhanya (3 years) y-m-d
Pushya Cancer	Vishakha Libra	Satabhisha Aquarius	
3°20'	20°00'	6°40'	3-00-00
4°00'	20°40'	7°20'	2-10-06
4°40'	21°20'	8°00'	2-08-12
5°20'	22°00'	8°40'	2-06-18
6°00'	22°40'	9°20'	2-04-24
6°40'	23°20'	10°00'	2-03-00
7°20'	24°00'	10°40'	2-01-06
8°00'	24°40'	11°20'	1-11-12
8°40'	25°20'	12°00'	1-09-18
9°20'	26°00'	12°40'	1-07-24
10°00'	26°40'	13°20'	1-06-00
10°40'	27°20'	14°00'	1-04-06
11°20'	28°00'	14°40'	1-02-12
12°00'	28°40'	15°20'	1-00-18
12°40'	29°20'	16°00'	0-10-24
13°20'	30°00'	16°40'	0-09-00
14°00'	Sco 0°40'	17°20'	0-07-06
14°40'	1°20'	18°00'	0-05-12
15°20'	2°00'	18°40'	0-03-18
16°00'	2°40'	19°20'	0-01-24
16°40'	3°20'	20°00'	0-00-00

BHADRIKA

Longitude of the Moon				Bhadrika (5 years) y-m-d
Bharani Aries	Magha Leo	Jyeshtha Scorpio	U. Bhadrapad Pisces	
13°20'	0°0'	16°40'	3°20'	5-00-00
14°00'	0°40'	17°20'	4°00'	4-09-00
14°40'	1°20'	18°00'	4°40'	4-06-00
15°20'	2°00'	18°40'	5°20'	4-03-00
16°00'	2°40'	19°20'	6°00'	4-00-00
16°40'	3°20'	20°00'	6°40'	3-09-00
17°20'	4°00'	20°40'	7°20'	3-06-00
18°00'	4°40'	21°20'	8°00'	3-03-00
18°40'	5°20'	22°00'	8°40'	3-00-00
19°20'	6°00'	22°40'	9°20'	2-09-00
20°00'	6°40'	23°20'	10°00'	2-06-00
20°40'	7°20'	24°00'	10°40'	2-03-00
21°20'	8°00'	24°40'	11°20'	2-00-00
22°00'	8°40'	25°20'	12°00'	1-09-00
22°40'	9°20'	26°00'	12°40'	1-06-00
23°20'	10°00'	26°40'	13°20'	1-03-00
24°00'	10°40'	27°20'	14°00'	1-00-00
24°40'	11°20'	28°00'	14°40'	0-09-00
25°20'	12°00'	28°40'	15°20'	0-06-00
26°00'	12°40'	29°20'	16°00'	0-03-00
26°40'	13°20'	30°00'	16°40	0-00-00

ULKA

Longitude of the Moon				Ulka (6 years) y-m-d
Krittika Aries	P. Bhadrapad Leo	Moola Sagittarius	Revati Pisces	
26°40'	13°20'	0°0'	16°40'	6-00-00
27°20'	14°00'	0°40'	17°20'	5-08-12
28°00'	14°40'	1°20'	18°00'	5-04-24
28°40'	15°20'	2°00'	18°40'	5-01-06
29°20'	16°00'	2°40'	19°20'	4-09-18
30°00'	16°40'	3°20'	20°00'	4-06-00
Tau0°40'	17°20'	4°00'	20°40'	4-02-12
1°20'	18°00'	4°40'	21°20'	4-10-24
2°00'	18°40'	5°20'	22°00'	3-07-06
2°40'	19°20'	6°00'	22°40'	3-03-18
3°20'	20°00'	6°40'	23°20'	3-00-00
4°00'	20°40'	7°20'	24°00'	2-08-12
4°40'	21°20'	8°00'	24°40'	2-04-24
5°20'	22°00'	8°40'	25°20'	2-01-06
6°00'	22°40'	9°20'	26°00'	1-09-18
6°40'	23°20'	10°00'	26°40'	1-06-00
7°20'	24°00'	10°40'	27°20'	1-02-12
8°00'	24°40'	11°20'	28°00'	0-10-24
8°40'	25°20'	12°00'	28°40'	0-07-06
9°20'	26°00'	12°40'	29°20'	0-03-18
10°00'	26°40'	13°20'	30°00'	0-00-00

SIDDHA

Longitude of the Moon			Siddha
Rohini Taurus	U. Phalguni Leo	P. Ashadha Sagittarius	(7 years) y-m-d
10°00'	26°40'	13°20'	7-00-00
10°40'	27°20'	14°00'	6-07-24
11°20'	28°00'	14°40'	6-03-18
12°00'	28°40'	15°20'	5-11-12
12°40'	29°20'	16°00'	5-07-06
13°20'	30°00'	16°40'	5-03-00
14°00'	Vir 0°40'	17°20'	4-10-24
14°40'	1°20'	18°00'	4-06-18
15°20'	2°00'	18°40'	4-02-12
16°00'	2°40'	19°20'	3-10-06
16°40'	3°20'	20°00'	3-06-00
17°20'	4°00'	20°40'	3-01-24
18°00'	4°40'	21°20'	2-09-18
18°40'	5°20'	22°00'	2-05-12
19°20'	6°00'	22°40'	2-01-06
20°00'	6°40'	23°20'	1-09-00
20°40'	7°20'	24°00'	1-04-24
21°20'	8°00'	24°40'	1-00-18
22°00'	8°40'	25°20'	0-08-12
22°40'	9°20'	26°00'	0-04-06
23°20'	10°00'	26°40'	0-00-00

SANKATA

Longitude of the Moon			Sankata
Mrigasira Taurus	Hasta Virgo	U. Ashadha Sagittarius	(8 years) y-m-d
23°20'	10°00'	26°40'	8-00-00
24°00'	10°40'	27°20'	7-07-06
24°40'	11°20'	28°00'	7-02-12
25°20'	12°00'	28°40'	6-09-18
26°00'	12°40'	29°20'	6-04-24
26°40'	13°20'	30°00'	6-00-00
27°20'	14°00'	Cap 0°40'	5-07-06
28°00'	14°40'	1°20'	5-02-12
28°40'	15°20'	2°00'	4-09-18
29°20'	16°00'	2°40'	4-04-24
30°00'	16°40'	3°20'	4-00-00
Gem 0°40'	17°20'	4°00'	3-07-06
1°20'	18°00'	4°40'	3-02-12
2°00'	18°40'	5°20'	2-09-18
2°40'	19°20'	6°00'	2-04-24
3°20'	20°00'	6°40'	2-00-00
4°00'	20°40'	7°20'	1-07-06
4°40'	21°20'	8°00'	1-02-12
5°20'	22°00'	8°40'	0-09-18
6°00'	22°40'	9°20'	0-04-24
6°40'	23°20'	10°00'	0-00-00

Table II-5 : Proportional parts of Yogini Dasha Balance

Nakshatramsha	Mangala Day	Mangala Hr	Mangala Min	Pingala Day	Pingala Hr	Pingala Min	Dhanya Day	Dhanya Hr	Dhanya Min	Bhramari Mth	Bhramari Day	Bhramari Hr	Bhramari Min	Bhadrika Mth	Bhadrika Day	Bhadrika Hr	Ulka Mth	Ulka Day	Ulka Hr	Ulka Min	Siddha Mth	Siddha Day	Siddha Hr	Sankata Mth	Sankata Day	Sankata Hr
1'	0	10	48	0	21	36	1	8	24	0	1	19	12	0	2	6	0	2	16	48	0	3	4	0	3	14
2'	0	21	36	1	19	12	2	16	48	0	3	14	24	0	4	12	0	5	9	36	0	6	7	0	7	5
3'	1	8	24	2	16	48	4	1	12	0	5	9	36	0	6	18	0	8	2	24	0	9	11	0	10	19
4'	1	19	12	3	14	24	5	9	36	0	7	4	48	0	9	0	0	10	19	12	0	12	14	0	14	10
5'	2	6	0	4	12	0	6	18	0	0	9	0	0	0	11	6	0	13	12	0	0	15	18	0	18	0
6'	2	16	48	5	9	36	8	2	24	0	10	19	12	0	13	12	0	16	4	48	0	18	22	0	21	14
7'	3	3	36	6	7	12	9	10	48	0	12	14	24	0	15	18	0	18	21	36	0	22	1	0	25	5
8'	3	14	24	7	4	48	10	19	12	0	14	9	36	0	18	0	0	21	14	24	0	25	5	0	28	19
9'	4	1	12	8	2	24	12	3	36	0	16	4	48	0	20	6	0	24	7	12	0	28	8	1	2	10
10'	4	12	0	9	0	0	13	12	0	0	18	0	0	0	22	12	0	27	0	0	1	1	12	1	6	0
11'	4	22	48	9	21	36	14	20	24	0	19	19	12	0	24	18	0	29	16	48	1	4	16	1	9	14
12'	5	9	36	10	19	12	16	4	48	0	21	14	24	0	27	0	1	2	9	36	1	7	19	1	13	5
13'	5	20	24	11	16	48	17	13	12	0	23	9	36	1	29	6	1	5	2	24	1	10	23	1	16	19
14'	6	7	12	12	14	24	18	21	36	0	25	4	48	1	1	12	1	7	19	12	1	14	2	1	20	10
15'	6	18	0	13	12	0	20	6	0	0	27	0	0	1	3	18	1	10	12	0	1	17	6	1	24	0
16'	7	4	48	14	9	36	21	14	24	0	28	19	12	1	6	0	1	13	4	48	1	20	10	1	27	14
17'	7	15	36	15	7	12	22	22	48	1	0	14	24	1	8	6	1	15	21	36	1	23	13	2	1	5
18'	8	2	24	16	4	48	24	7	12	1	2	9	36	1	10	12	1	18	14	24	1	26	17	2	4	19
19'	8	13	12	17	2	24	25	15	36	1	4	4	48	1	12	18	1	21	7	12	1	29	20	2	8	10
20'	9	0	0	18	0	0	27	0	0	1	6	0	0	1	15	0	1	24	0	0	2	3	0	2	12	0

Table II-6 : Yogini Dasha Major and Sub Periods

Yogini	Mangala (1y)		Pingala (2 y)		Dhanya (3y)		Bhramari (4y)		Bhadrika (5y)		Ulka (6y)		Siddha (7y)		Sankata (8y)	
Sub periods	S.P. y-m-d	Total y-m-d	S.P. y-m-d	Total y-m-d	S.P. y-m-d	Total y-m-d	S.P. y-m-d	Total y-m-d	S.P. y-m-d	Total y-m-d	S.P. y-m-d	Total y-m-d	S.P. y-m-d	Total y-m-d	S.P. y-m-d	Total y-m-d
Mangala	0-0-10	0-0-10	–	–	–	–	–	–	–	–	–	–	–	–	–	–
Pingala	0-0-20	0-1-00	0-1-10	0-1-10	–	–	–	–	–	–	–	–	–	–	–	–
Dhanya	0-1-00	0-2-00	0-2-00	0-3-10	0-3-0	0-3-0	–	–	–	–	–	–	–	–	–	–
Bhramari	0-1-10	0-3-10	0-2-20	0-6-00	0-4-0	0-7-0	0-5-10	0-5-10	–	–	–	–	–	–	–	–
Bhadrika	0-1-20	0-5-00	0-3-10	0-9-10	0-5-0	1-0-0	0-6-20	1-0-0	0-8-10	0-8-10	–	–	–	–	–	–
Ulka	0-2-00	0-7-00	0-4-00	1-1-10	0-6-0	1-6-0	0-8-00	1-8-0	0-10-00	1-6-10	1-0-0	1-0-0	–	–	–	–
Siddha	0-2-10	0-9-10	0-4-20	1-6-00	0-7-0	2-1-0	0-9-10	2-5-10	0-11-20	2-6-00	1-2-0	2-2-0	1-4-10	1-4-10	–	–
Sankata	0-2-20	1-0-00	0-5-10	1-11-10	0-8-0	2-9-0	0-10-20	3-4-0	1-1-10	3-7-10	1-4-0	3-6-0	1-6-20	2-11-00	1-9-10	1-9-10
Mangala	–	–	0-0-20	2-0-00	0-1-0	2-10-0	0-1-10	3-5-10	0-1-20	3-9-00	0-2-0	3-8-0	0-2-10	3-1-10	0-2-20	2-0-00
Pingala	–	–	–	–	0-2-0	3-0-0	0-2-20	3-8-0	0-3-10	4-0-10	0-4-0	4-0-0	0-4-20	3-6-00	0-5-10	2-5-10
Dhanya	–	–	–	–	–	–	0-4-00	4-0-0	0-5-00	4-5-10	0-6-0	4-6-0	0-7-00	4-1-00	0-8-00	3-1-10
Bhramari	–	–	–	–	–	–	–	–	0-6-20	5-0-00	0-8-0	5-2-0	0-9-10	4-10-10	0-10-20	4-0-00
Bhadrika	–	–	–	–	–	–	–	–	–	–	0-10-0	6-0-0	0-11-20	5-10-00	1-1-10	5-1-10
Ulka	–	–	–	–	–	–	–	–	–	–	–	–	1-2-00	7-0-00	1-4-00	6-5-10
Siddha	–	–	–	–	–	–	–	–	–	–	–	–	–	–	1-6-20	8-0-00

Step 3

The increase in the minutes of the longitude of the Moon from the nearest lower figure mentioned in Table II-4 is referred to in Table II-5 under the relevant dasha. The period mentioned there is to be *subtracted* from the balance of dasha noted in Step 2.

Step 4

Adding the corrected balance of dasha to the date of birth gives the date when the dasha operative at birth will end. The next dasha will be according to the cyclic order of the Yoginis. Table II-6 gives the sub-periods of Yoginis in the major period of all Yoginis.

Example

A native was born on January 27, 1960 at 23:01 hrs. IST at Ferozepore, Punjab, India (Lat. 30°55'N, Long. 74°36'E). The Moon is in Capricorn 6°12'. Now proceed to calculate the Yogini dasha:

Step 1 : Refer to Table II-3. Capricorn 6°12' indicates that the native was born in Sankata dasha.

Step 2 : Refer to Table II-4 under Sankata dasha. The nearest lower figure to the longitude of the Moon is Capricorn 6°00'. The balance of dasha is 2-4-24 (indicating 2 years - 4 months - 24 days).

Step 3 : The difference between longitude of the Moon (Capricorn 6°12') and nearest lower figure (Capricorn 6°00') is 12'. Twelve minutes under Sankata dasha in Table II-5 gives a balance of 1 month-13 days-5 hours. *Subtracting* this period from the balance of dasha gives the corrected balance of dasha.

		y	m	d	h
Balance of Sankata		2	4	24	0
Difference of 12'	(–)		1	13	5
Corrected balance		2	3	10	19

Step 4 : Adding the corrected balance of Sankata dasha to the date of birth gives the date when Sankata dasha ends and next dasha, Mangala, begins. The major periods of dashas are added till the present running period which in this case falls under Ulka dasha. The sub-periods of Ulka are derived from Table II-6. The first sub-period in the major period of Ulka will also be of Ulka. The subsequent sub-periods will be of Siddha, Sankata, Mangala, Pingala, Dhanya, etc., in the regular order.

The order of dashas will be as follows:

	y	m	d
Date of Birth	1960	1	27
Bal. of Sankata	2	3	10
	1962	5	7

First Cycle of Yogini Dasha

Yogini	dasha period		Date y	m	d	Native Age
Sankata	2y-3m-10d	ends	1962	5	7	2y-3m
Mangala	1 year	ends	1963	5	7	3y-3m
Pingala	2 years	ends	1965	5	7	5y-3m
Dhanya	3 years	ends	1968	5	7	8y-3m
Bhramari	4 years	ends	1972	5	7	12y-3m
Bhadrika	5 years	ends	1977	5	7	17y-3m
Ulka	6 years	ends	1983	5	7	23y-3m
Siddha	7 years	ends	1990	5	7	30y-3m
Sankata	5y-8m-20d	ends	1996	1	27	36y-0m

Second Cycle of Yogini Dasha

Yogini	dasha period		Date y	m	d	Native Age
Sankata	2y-3m-10d	ends	1998	5	7	38y-3m
Mangala	1 year	ends	1999	5	7	39y-3m
Pingala	2 years	ends	2001	5	7	41y-3m
Dhanya	3 years	ends	2004	5	7	44y-3m
Bhramari	4 years	ends	2008	5	7	48y-3m
Bhadrika	5 years	ends	2013	5	7	53y-3m
Ulka	6 years	ends	2019	5	7	59y-3m
Siddha	7 years	ends	2026	5	7	66y-3m
Sankata	5y-8m-20d	ends	2032	1	27	72y-0m

Sub-periods in the major period of Ulka (Second cycle)

Yogini Major and Sub-period	dasha period y-m-d		Date y	m	d
Ulka-Ulka		begins	2013	5	7
	1-0-0	ends	2014	5	7
Ulka-Siddha	1-2-0	ends	2015	7	7
Ulka-Sankata	1-4-0	ends	2016	11	7
Ulka-Mangala	0-2-0	ends	2017	1	7
Ulka-Pingala	0-4-0	ends .	2017	5	7
Ulka-Dhanya	0-6-0	ends	2017	11	7
Ulka-Bhramari	0-8-0	ends	2018	7	7
Ulka-Bhadrika	0-10-0	ends	2019	5	7

CHAPTER THREE

THE BASIC PRINCIPLES

For a quick reference some of the basic principles of Vedic astrology are being given here so that a new entrant into the fold of this system may also grasp how the Yogini dasha is to be applied.

Planetary Significations

The Sun

Soul, self, father, king, government, authority, royalty or royal favour, fire or electricity, politics, right eye, east.

The Moon

Mother, motherland, emotions, mental inclination, royalty, name and fame, facial lustre, women, liquids, pearls, silver, milk, north-west.

Mars

Younger brothers or sisters, stamina, courage, anger, violence, accidents, injury, surgery, enemies, police, armed forces, doctors, land or immovable properties, south.

Mercury

Intelligence, speech, education, communication, business, mathematics, astrology, writing, middleman, dance, drama, imitation or mimicry, friends, maternal uncle, nervous system, skin, north.

Jupiter

Children, elder brothers and sisters, wisdom, learning, devotion to gods, holy places, scriptures, judges, wealth, expansion, minister, teacher, guru, priest, liver, north-east.

Venus

Wife, spouse, sexual matters, vehicles, arts, singing, poetry, scents, jewellery or precious stones, luxury or luxurious articles, beauty, places of entertainment, chemicals, buying and selling, genital organs, kidney, south-east.

Saturn

Longevity, laziness, death, sorrow, adversity, poverty, sickness, black products, separation or renunciation, service, servants, elderly persons, chronic diseases, strangulation, cruel deeds, west.

Rahu

Paternal grandfather, harsh speech, gambling, outcasts, foreigners, confusion, poison, snakebite, widow, pilgrimage, acute or sharp pain, south-west.

Ketu

Maternal grandfather, salvation, spiritual *sadhana*, hyper-sensitivity, mathematical ability, sudden mishaps, foreign language, genius, dips in sacred waters, witchcraft, leather, south-east.

Planetary Strength

Planets become strong or weak according to their disposition in birth chart and other divisional charts. A planet can achieve strength from different sources which is measured by detailed Shadabala calculations. For a quick evaluation, a planet is considered strong under the following conditions:

(a) in exaltation sign

(b) in moolatrikona sign

(c) in own sign

(d) in a friend's sign

(e) lord of a benefic house

(f) associated or aspected by benefics or lords of benefic houses

(g) *Vargottama* (a planet in the same sign in Navamsha as in the birth chart)

(h) *Aarohi* (a planet moving towards its sign of exaltation)

(i) directionally strong*

(j) having improved its position in divisional charts compared to birth chart.

A planet is considered weak under in following conditions:

(a) in debilitation sign

(b) in enemy's sign

(c) lordship of a malefic house

(d) associated or aspected by malefics or lords of malefic houses

(e) combust (close proximity with the Sun)

(f) directionally weak

(g) *Avarohi* (a planet moving towards its sign of debilitation)

---

* A planet is considered strong if it acquires a particular direction in a horoscope. Mercury and Jupiter in lagna; the Moon and Venus in fourth house; Saturn in seventh house and the Sun and Mars in the tenth house are considered to have full directional strength. Planets being seventh from the above positions — Mercury and Jupiter in seventh house; the Moon and Venus in tenth house; Saturn in lagna and the Sun and Mars in fourth house — are directionally weak.

(h) having deteriorated its position in divisional charts compared to birth chart

(i) in Rashi-Sandhi or *Gandanta**

Significations of Houses

Lagna or First House

Body, complexion, health, nature, longevity, general happiness.

Second House

Accumulated wealth or valuables like jewellery, precious stones, etc., family, food, speech, longevity of spouse or the longevity of marriage (being eighth from the seventh house), death, right eye.

Third House

Valour, co-borns (younger brothers and sisters), efforts, short journeys, inherent talent, writings, communicative skill, longevity of parents, servants or subordinates, friends, neighbours, reason of death, right ear, shoulder, upper limb.

Fourth House

Mother, residence, parental house, property, lands, conveyances, cattle, comforts or luxuries, domestic happiness, happiness of all sorts, masses, parliament, profession of the spouse (tenth from the seventh house), chest.

Fifth House

Children, intellect, aptitude, education, knowledge of scriptures, emotions, dignity (dignified position), fall from

---

* The point where one sign ends and the other sign begins is known as Rashi-sandhi. Rashi-sandhi of Cancer-Leo, Scorpio-Sagittarius and Pisces-Aries is called Gandanta as it is the end of a sign as well as a group of nine nakshatras.

status, change or break in profession (eighth from the tenth house), accumulated karmas of previous lives, upper abdomen.

Sixth House

Enemy, disease, resistance to disease, disputes, legal cases, loss (eighth from the eleventh house of gains), accidents, fear, stamina to fight back, difficulties, competition, struggle, maternal uncle, debts or loans, service aptitude, contract, domestic pets, waist.

Seventh House

Marriage, spouse (life partner), sexual aberrations, business partner, trading, journey, attainment of position or post (tenth from the tenth house), public image, death, pelvis, pelvic organs (rectum, urinary bladder, uterus and ovaries).

Eighth House

Longevity, sudden fall, secret part or aspect of life, wealth of the spouse, disgrace, scandals, break or change, unorthodoxy, place and mode of death, inheritance, adjustment in the married life, controversy, private parts.

Ninth House

Father, luck, religious aptitude, guru or master, teacher, overseas travels, sisters or brothers of spouse, hips, and thighs.

Tenth House

Occupation or profession, status, professional excellence, source of livelihood, government, mother of spouse, knee joints.

Eleventh House

Gains, achievements, honours, titles, elder brothers and sisters, accidents (sixth from sixth house), spouse of the first child (seventh from the fifth), left ear, legs.

Twelfth House

Expenditure on good or bad account, investment, loss, foreign country, hospitalization, final emancipation, bed pleasures, separation, renunciation, confinement, left eye, feet.

Significator Planets for the Twelve Houses

First House   : The Sun, the Moon.

Second House   : Jupiter for wealth,
                          Mercury for speech.

Third House   : Mars for co-borns and valour,
                          Saturn for servants and subordinates.

Fourth House   : The Moon for mother,
                          Venus for conveyances,
                          Mars for lands and properties.

Fifth House   : Jupiter for children,
                          Mercury for education.

Sixth House   : Mars for accidents,
                          Saturn for sickness,
                          Mercury for enemies and
                          maternal relations.

Seventh House : Venus for spouse.

Eighth House   : Saturn for longevity.

Ninth House   : Sun for father,
                          Jupiter for guru, teacher or religion.

Tenth House   : Sun for profession.

Eleventh House : Jupiter for elder brothers and sisters,
                          Sun for gains.

Twelfth House   : Saturn for separation or renunciation,
                          Venus for bed pleasures,
                          Ketu for emancipation.

Houses to be considered for different significations

Relations

Father	:	The Sun and the ninth house from the Sun.
Mother	:	The Moon and the fourth house from the Moon.
Younger brothers and sisters	:	Mars and the third house from Mars.
Elder brothers and sisters	:	Jupiter and the eleventh house from Jupiter.
Spouse	:	Venus and the seventh house from Venus.
Children	:	Jupiter and the fifth house from Jupiter.
Maternal Uncle	:	Mercury and the sixth house from Mercury.

Others

Lands and properties	:	Mars and the fourth house from Mars.
Luxuries and conveyances	:	Venus and the fourth house from Venus.
Education	:	Mercury and the fifth house from Mercury.
Sickness, enemy	:	Mercury and sixth from Mercury
Longevity	:	Saturn and the eighth house from Saturn.

Maraka Houses and Planets

The eighth house from the lagna is the house of longevity. The eighth *from the eighth house* is the third house, an alternative house of longevity. Twelfth from any house causes loss to that house. In this case twelfth from third and eighth houses are second and seventh houses respectively, which cause loss of longevity, and, therefore, they are called death inflicting houses or maraka houses.

The seventh and the second lords also become the killer or maraka planet. The planets posited in the maraka houses, with the killer planets, and the planets aspected by the killer planets also attain death inflicting powers and become marakas or killer planets.

The lord of the twelfth house is also considered a maraka. Saturn is the unconditional maraka for any lagna. Rahu, if placed in sixth, eighth or twelfth house also becomes maraka.

CHAPTER FOUR

INTERPRETATION OF A HOROSCOPE

Judgement of a horoscopic chart comprises of manifold analysis of different houses of the birth chart. The judgement being the final outcome, the process in itself consists of many steps. To simplify the process, it can be divided into following stages:

(1) General assessment of the birth chart by the strength of the lagna, the Moon and the Sun.

(2) Assessment of the kendras and trikonas.

(3) Distribution of planets in the four groups – *Dharma, Artha, Kaama* and *Moksha* indicates the inclination of the native.

(4) Check the concentration or the distribution of the planets in a particular area of the chart. This gives an idea about the type of the horoscope.

(5) Judge the disposition of the different house lords. More carefully, check their inter-connection.

(6) Check the different yogas or combinations present in the horoscope.

(7) Judge the interrelation of the houses and their lords, to assess the horoscope deeply.

(8) Check the dasha pattern the native is getting. This unfolds the life pattern in a systematic way. This also helps to time the events.

Stages of Analysis Discussed in Detail

General Assessment

The personality of an individual is dependent on the strength of the lagna lord and influence of planets on the lagna of the horoscopic chart. The Moon represents the mental makeup of the native. Association or aspect of planets on the Moon influences the temperament of the native according to the qualities of the influencing planet.

Affliction of the lagna, adverse placement of the lagna lord and the Moon, and association or aspect of malefic planets is an adverse combination for the health of the native. Under such conditions, the dashas operating in the early childhood should be watched carefully.

Maharshi Parashara has described the use of *Sudarshana Chakra* for the purpose of synthesising the results of the three lagnas (i) the lagna of the birth chart; (ii) the Moon lagna; and (iii) the Sun lagna.

Check the lagna and its lord to assess the physical well-being of the native, the Moon and its sign to judge the mental makeup of the native, and finally the Sun for the strength of the soul. All three factors given above, if studied in depth, will give the best available picture of the native's life. To ignore this vital first step and predict solely on the basis of good or bad yogas in the birth chart is to run into disaster.

Assessment of the Kendras and Trikonas

The strength of the birth chart also depends upon the kendras or quadrants. All the kendras being occupied by the planets, specially by benefics, give additional thrust to the horoscope. Benefics here increase the longevity of the native, and the malefics affect the longevity adversely.

The four kendras represent the four important fronts of life, namely:

1st House - Self

4th House - Family, happiness and resources

7th House - Married life, or public life, alternatively

10th House - *Karma* or occupation.

Disposition of the planets in the above houses, whether good or bad, affect the life pattern of the native in a big way.

Trikonas or trines are the protective shield for the native. The fifth house is the house of the accumulated good or bad *karmas*; and the ninth house, the house of religious deeds. In times of disaster, only these houses play their role to give their benign protection. Benefics in the trikonas are praised by the classical texts. Lagna being both a kendra and a trikona becomes doubly important here.

Distribution of Planets in four groups

An important grouping of the houses of a horoscopic chart is according to the four distinctive factors of life – *Dharma* (religious deeds), *Artha* (materialistic pursuits), *Kaama* (sexual indulgence) and *Moksha* (spiritual development).

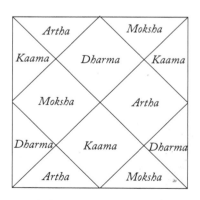

	Houses		
Dharma (Religious deeds)	: 1	5	9
Artha (Materialistic pursuits)	: 2	6	10
Kaama (Sexual indulgence)	: 3	7	11
Moksha (Spiritual development)	: 4	8	12

A glance at the concentration and distribution of planets in these four groups in the horoscopic chart of an individual indicates the inherent nature and inclination of the person in his life.

Concentration or the Distribution of Planets in different houses

This gives an idea about the chief activity in the life of the native. For example, concentration of the planets in the tenth house of a birth chart will keep the native busy in his work in the majority of years of his life and he may not be able to give full attention to other spheres of life. In the same way, concentration of the planets along 6-12 axis of the horoscope may keep him sick or he may be engaged in hard work or run through difficulties, etc.

Too much concentration of malefic planets along a particular house or axis creates tension or difficulties in that area and the placement of benefics give a positive view of that aspect of life. This can be used to highlight the area of achievement and the area of misery in the life of the native.

Too much concentration of planets in only a few houses of the horoscope also creates an imbalance of sorts. It indicates that certain areas of life of the individual are more distinctly represented than others. A wider distribution of planets in the horoscope produces a more balanced individual.

Analysis of Individual Houses

The key to interpretation of a horoscopic chart lies in the assessment of the strengths and weaknesses of different houses of the horoscope. A sum total of the twelve houses of a horoscope is what indicates all the areas in the life of an individual. The strength or weakness of a house will influence the results attributed to that particular house.

Planets tend to provide important links amongst the different houses. There are four ways by which a house or house lord can have a relationship with another house or house lord:

34

Position

A house lord placed in another house will establish a relationship by its position in that house.

Aspect

A planet aspecting a house will form a relationship between the house of which it is the owner and the house which it aspects.

Conjunction

When two house lords are placed together in any of the houses of a horoscope, the relationship is due to the conjunction of these house lords, in addition to their relationship with the house in which they conjoin.

Exchange

A fourth link between two houses is established when their lords are involved in an exchange (Parivartan yoga). This is further elaborated hereunder a little later.

The quality, quantity and nature of results are dependent upon the combined result of the disposition of the three factors, namely:
- the house
- the house lord, and
- the *karaka* or significator.

House

The house is influenced either by placement or by aspect of planets. Influence by the lord of a malefic house or by natural malefics will adversely influence the results ascribed to that house. Similarly placement or aspect of benefics or lords of benefic houses enhances the results of the house concerned. Placement of the house lord in its own house protects the house and it will always improve the results of that house.

House Lord

Disposition of the house lord in one of the trines or kendras gives positive results while placement in *Trik sthanas* (6th, 8th or 12th) houses is a negative factor for the house.

Karaka

Ill disposed, weak or afflicted significator gives trouble to the areas indicated by the significator. A house indicates various results but to differentiate between them, the use of significators or *karakas* becomes important. For example, affliction to the fourth house may not mean an affliction to everything signified by the fourth house, i.e., mother, conveyances or lands. Disposition of the related significator will have the final bearing on the assessment of the fourth house. Moon if afflicted will trouble the mother, Venus the conveyances, and Mars the lands, and so on.

A deep analysis of these three factors – the house, the house lord and karaka – will indicate whether the results attributed to the house will be negative or positive and also the extent to which they will be adverse or favourable. Relevant divisional charts play a pivotal role in the final outcome of the results.

Yogas

The interrelationship of nine planets and the twelve houses will make numerous combinations or yogas. These yogas can be broadly classified into three main categories: Rajayoga or yogas for prosperity, fame and success in life; Dhana yoga or yogas producing wealth; and Arishta yoga or yogas resulting in ill-health and penury.

In addition, two more factors need to be considered:

(i) Parivartana yogas or exchanges of house lords, and

(ii) Special features in a horoscope.

Raja Yogas

The word 'Raja' literally means the king, and the power and authority flowing from him. In the olden context these were the combinations used to predict the attainment of power by the kings; in the modern context, these combinations are now applicable to any sphere of activity in life. The more the number of Raja yogas present in a particular horoscope, the more elevated the status of the person.

There are many Raja yogas given in the classical texts. The essence of them can be put in the following way:

The kendras or quadrants are the *Vishnu Sthanas* and the trikonas or trines are the *Lakshmi Sthanas*. Any interrelation of their house lords with each other by way of position, aspect or conjunction (or even exchange) will produce a Raja yoga.

The houses where the above combinations take place are benefitted the most. The houses whose lords are involved in the above Raja yogas are also benefitted.

Dhana Yogas

The second house is the house of accumulated wealth and eleventh house the house of gains. The trikonas – the first, the fifth and the ninth houses – are known as *Lakshmi Sthanas* or the adobe of Goddess of wealth, Lakshmi. The lords of the 2nd and 11th houses and those of the trikonas due to their interrelationship by way of position, aspect, conjunction or exchange, give rise to Dhana yogas which are conducive to acquisition as well as accumulation of wealth. Much wealth is promised in the birth chart if several unblemished Dhana yogas are formed in benefic houses.

Arishta Yogas

The *Trik sthanas* (sixth, eighth and twelfth houses) and their lords generally produce misery with few exceptions operable under certain special conditions only.

The lord of any house, by getting connected to one or more of the above houses, produces evil results with respect to that house. For example, the fifth lord if placed in the eighth house, with the sixth lord, and aspected by the twelfth lord, will produce the worst results to the children of the native, and so on.

Parivartana Yogas

It is a mode of interconnection of the houses or their lords in a better way. For example if the 2nd lord is in the 11th house and the 11th lord is in the 2nd house it is a better Dhana yoga. Similarly if there is an exchange between the lagna and the 10th house, it will be a very good combination for fame, a Raja yoga.

If such an exchange takes place between the fourth and the fifth lord, it will be especially good for the education as both the above houses are connected with learning.

Special Features

It is imperative on the part of an astrologer to identify any striking features in the horoscope. These may be good or bad, but they do have their effect on the complete judgement of the horoscope.

For example, if the birth of the native takes place when the Moon is in the Gandanta (certain dangerous positions), the other benefic yogas present may not give results to their fullest potential.

Or, if the birth of the native takes place in the Abhijit Muhurta (birth at mid-day or mid-night), the other malefic yogas present in the horoscope will not be so much dreaded and the native will enjoy a good life.

A combined, overall view of all the above yogas will give an idea about the positive or negative outlook of the horoscope, which in most of the cases is a mixture of the above.

Deeper assessment of the horoscope needs thinking and re-thinking on the part of the astrologer. This thinking will give new meanings to the different combinations present in the horoscope. Here the astrologer imparts different modifications and innovations to the accepted classical principles and applies them in the present context. With the combined use of the above steps of analysis, one is able to analyse the birth chart. This gives a feel of the horoscope, a picture of the life of the native. To time the above events, foreseen by the in-depth analysis, is the next stage of the analysis.

Dashas Pattern: To Time the Events

The dasha pattern or sequence of dashas that the native gets in his life influences him in a very peculiar and specific way.

A good dasha operating at the right time can altogether change the pattern of the native's life.

A person can have few dreaded combinations present in his horoscope but may not experience them as the concerned dasha may not operate in his lifetime.

So the dasha sequence gives the time of the fructification of the events and a good career-making dasha, if ill-timed, may not benefit the native in the expected way.

Example Horoscope

Let us briefly analyse a horoscope in the light of some of the above mentioned principles. We shall take up the chart of Angelina Jolie, a beautiful personality from the film world who is also engaged in numerous social and charitable activities the world over. She was born on June 4, 1975 at 9:09 hours at Los Angeles, CA, USA.

I. Strength from the lagna, the Moon and the Sun

Cancer lagna with the benevolent Venus close to the degree of the lagna, and the lagna lord Moon, associating with

Jupiter Moon Mars		Mer (R) Sun Ketu	Saturn
	Angelina Jolie 4 June, 1975 9:09 am Los Angeles, CA		⟋Lagna 5°22' Venus 4°27'
	Rahu		

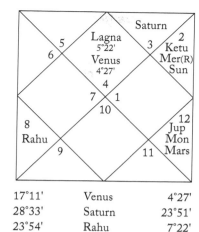

Lagna	5°22'	Mars	17°11'	Venus	4°27'
Sun	19°46'	Mercury (R)	28°33'	Saturn	23°51'
Moon	19°33'	Jupiter	23°54'	Rahu	7°22'

the fifth and the ninth lords in the ninth house, with the additional aspect of Jupiter on the lagna confers on the native rare benevolence, beauty and sensitivity. Saturn's aspect from the twelfth house instills seriousness and the urge to serve those in need.

From the Moon, three important and friendly planets occupy the lagna; these are the lagna lord Jupiter, the fifth lord Moon and the ninth lord Mars, again forming a rare and potent raja-yoga. The aspect of the eleventh and twelfth lord Saturn from the fourth house on this yoga confers recognition, seriousness and a charitable disposition.

From the Sun, the lagna is occupied by the fourth lord Sun and the second and fifth lord Mercury, and there is a strong eleventh house receiving the aspect of the yoga-karaka Saturn from the second house, conferring a strong combination of wealth. Rahu in the seventh house confers on her an unconventional approach in matters pertaining to relationships whose multiplicity is indicated by the placement of the seventh lord Mars in the eleventh house, in association with the eleventh lord Jupiter, which as the eighth lord also brings in suffering in relationships.

II. Kendras and trikonas

Only Venus, the most benevolent, soft and artistic planet, occupies the lagna close to the degree of the lagna so that it remains in the lagna in several divisional charts, conferring on her a rare charm and beauty. The other Kendras are unoccupied and remain mainly unafflicted. Their lords are also well placed except the seventh lord Saturn which occupies the twelfth house and is aspected by Mars. Mars and Saturn mutually aspect each other.

The trikonas receive mixed influence of benefics and malefic though the benefic influences predominate.

III. Distribution of planets

It will be seen that all the planets in the chart occupy the visible half of the horoscope (from houses 7 to 1). This ensures that the native is active in public life, is well known around the globe and her slightest action is subjected to public scrutiny.

Looked at in a different manner, there is predominance of planets in the ninth house (*Dharma*, benevolence) and the eleventh house (*Kama*, physical indulgence). Both aspects are predominant in the native. In addition, Venus in the lagna is in the *Dharma* house. Saturn in the twelfth house (*Moksha*, service) prompts her to indulge in charity and social work.

IV. Inter-connection of different house lords, yogas, etc.

All the trikona lords join together in the most powerful trikona, the ninth house, forming a highly potent raja-yoga. The yoga forming in the ninth house is a combination of several different raja-yogas: The Moon conjoined with Jupiter (Gaja-Kesari yoga), lagna lord and the fifth lord together (raja-yoga), lagna lord and the ninth lord together (raja-yoga), lagna lord and the tenth lord in the ninth house (raja-yoga), fifth lord joining the ninth lord (raja-yoga), ninth and tenth lords in the ninth house (raja-yoga), etc.

The chart has indications for some wayward behavior also. The native had a tendency to injure herself during her early years and some interest in drugs. The tendency to self-mutilation manifested in later years too, in a much modified and reformed way when she chose to have her breasts, and subsequently also her ovaries, removed in order to pre-empt the development of a likely cancer. The fifth house of thinking is involved in Rahu-Ketu axis as also is Mercury, the planet of reasoning. The fifth lord Mars associates with the sixth lord Jupiter and is aspected by the eighth lord Saturn from the twelfth house. The Moon shares the same planetary influences as does Mars. The role of Jupiter is the saving grace.

She has done remarkable social and humanitarian work to earn recognition from the United Nations High Commissioner for Refugees (UNHCR). The twelfth lord (service, humanitarian work, charity) Mercury in the eleventh aspects the fifth house of thinking. The discerning reader may also note that, other than Venus, all the remaining planets have something to do with her fifth house or fifth lord. In whatever she undertakes, she puts all her heart into it.

V. Yogini dasha

We shall take up only some events of her life to indicate that the Yogini dasha is a highly reliable tool when applied to a horoscope to time the events.

Beginning of Career

She began professional carrer in 1993: Yogini dasha was Sankata (Rahu) in fifth house of dignity and its dispositor Mars, also lord of the tenth house of profession, forms an excellent raja-yoga in the ninth house.

Professional Breakthrough

Professional breakthrough during the years 1998 to 2000. She was running the major period of Dhanya (Jupiter) from February 1998 to February 2001. Jupiter influences fifth house and forms excellent raja-yogas in the ninth house along with tenth lord Mars and lagna lord Moon.

Summary of the Events

Event	Yogini Dasha	Relationship
Begining of career 1993	Sankata (Rahu) Feb.'87 - Feb.'95	Dispositor Mars, also 10th lord of profession with lagna and 9th lords
Professional breakthrough 1998-2000 Career advancement 2001-2005	Dhanya (Jupiter) Feb.'98 - Feb.'01 Bhramari (Mars) Feb.'01 - Feb.'05	Jupiter with 10th lord and lagna lord Yogakaraka Mars is 10th lord
Goodwill ambassador Aug. 27, 2001	Bhramari-Bhadrika (Mars-Mercury)	Mercury - 3rd lord (communications), 12th lord (foreign)
Bilateral breast removal Feb. 16, 2013	Ulka-Sankata (Saturn-Rahu)	Saturn - in 12th (hospitalization) Rahu - disp. Mars with lagna lord
Marriage to Brad Pitt Aug. 23, 2014	Ulka-Bhramari (Saturn-Mars)	Saturn - 7th lord Mars - aspected by 7th lord Saturn
Bilateral ovary removal March 2015	Ulka-Bhramari (Saturn-Mars)	Saturn and Mars indicate surgery involving removal of body parts

Role of Sankata (Rahu) in her life:

1976	Parent's separation	Ulka-Sankata	Saturn-*Rahu*
1994	Depression	Sankata	*Rahu*
1997	Attempted suicide	Pingala-Sankata	Sun-*Rahu*
2008	Birth of twins	Bhadrika-Sankata	Mercury-*Rahu*
2013	Surgery	Ulka-Sankata	Saturn-*Rahu*

More recognition in the dasha of Bhramari (Mars) from February 2001 to February 2005. Mars, a yogakaraka (owner of a kendra and a trikona), is involved in raja-yogas.

Goodwill Ambassador

UNHCR Goodwill Ambassador, August 27, 2001: Bhramari-Bhadrika (Mars-Mercury). Mercury is the third lord of communications and twelfth lord of overseas, in the eleventh house of achievements and recognition. She continues her humanitarian work and has earned recognition, appreciation and awards for her work.

Boy friend at teenage

Boy friend at fourteen: Dasha was Sankata (February 1987 to February 1995), Rahu in the fifth house (fascination). Its dispositor is in a mutual aspect with the seventh lord Saturn in the twelfth house (bed pleasures).

Marriage

Marriage to Brad Pitt, August 23, 2014: Ulka-Bhramari (Saturn-Mars). Saturn is the seventh lord (marriage/relationship) and Mars the fifth lord (fascination).

Surgeries

Bilateral breast removal, February 16, 2013: Ulka-Sankata (Saturn-Rahu). Saturn (removal of a body organ/amputation) in the twelfth house (hospitalization) aspects the Moon (karaka for breast) and is located in the fourth house (breast) from the Moon. Influence of Mars on both the Moon and Saturn indicates surgery. Rahu is in the fifth house, in the sixth house (surgery) from the mahadasha lord Saturn, and its dispositor Mars is with the Moon, aspected by Saturn.

Bilateral ovary removal, March 2015: Ulka-Bhramari (Saturn-Mars). Both Saturn and Mars indicate surgery involving removal of a body organ. Saturn as the seventh lord represents internal genital organs (ovaries) of a woman.

Role of Sankata in her life

It has already been pointed out that all grahas, other than Venus, have something to do with either the fifth house or the fifth lord in the chart of Angelina Jolie. The fifth house thus becomes pre-eminent in her chart. She happens to be a highly sensitive individual who puts all her heart into whatever she undertakes. Rahu in the fifth house represents the Yogini Sankata. It is no wonder that several significant events in her life have occurred during the mahadasha or antardasha of Sankata. We enumerate a few of them.

Separation of parents, 1976: Ulka (Saturn)-Sankata (Rahu). Saturn is the eighth lord, located in the fourth house *from the Moon* (karaka for mother), aspecting the ninth house and ninth lord (father). Saturn and Rahu are 6-8 from each other precipitating in an unpleasant event.

Depression, 1994: Sankata (Rahu). Malefic in the fifth house causes mental anguish and related sufferings, especially when the fifth lord as well as the Moon are under the influence of the sixth and the eighth lords.

Attempted suicide, 1997: Pingala (Sun)-Sankata (Rahu). Fifth house in the Rahu-Ketu axis (RKA) aspected by the Sun and retrograde Mercury, and the Moon (karaka for the mind) as well as the fifth lord Mars (thinking, mental status) under the influence of the sixth lord as well as the eighth lord are enough to disturb the mental balance of the native with a tendency to self-harm.

Birth of twins, 2008: Bhadrika (Mercury)-Sankata (Rahu). Rahu is in the fifth house while Mercury aspects the fifth house. The aspect of Jupiter on the fifth house and its association with the fifth lord provide the promise for progeny.

Surgery, 2013: Ulka (Saturn)-Sankata (Rahu). Placed in the 6-8 position from each other, involving houses five (mental suffering, major health event) and twelve (hospitalization), with lordship of eighth house (amputation, removal of a body organ) by Saturn (itself a malefic, indicating surgery involving removal of a body organ), this dasha ensures that she goes for a major surgery (bilateral mastectomy) where some body organ (both breasts in this case) is amputated. Earlier, during her childhood, the first cycle of Ulka-Sankata had caused a separation of her parents. The same Saturn ensured removal of both her ovaries in a later dasha, Ulka (Saturn)-Bhramari (Mars), in the year 2015.

It will thus be noted that every time her Sankata dasha (major or sub-) operated, some event pertaining to her fifth house manifested. Her next Sankata major-period will be from February 2023 to February 2031.

It may be noted that we have not considered any divisional charts in this analysis. Use of divisional charts in any serious astrological analysis is mandatory. Combined with the Vimshottari dasha, the Yogini dasha would give excellent results. We exhort the reader to take this whole chapter seriously in order to enhance the success rate of his predictions.

CHAPTER FIVE

INTERPRETATION OF DIVISIONAL CHARTS

The uniqueness of Vedic a strology lies in its versatility of techniques. Like the dasha systems, divisional charts constitute one such technique which outshines any other system of astrology in the world.

While the dashas are meant for the timing of events, the divisional charts or vargas are meant to find out the promise inherent in a horoscope in great details. A complete analysis of the horoscopic chart involves first ascertaining the inherent promise in the chart through the study of the birth chart and its divisional charts, and then timing the likely events through an analysis of the dashas.

The extent of one sign is divided into various parts. The lagna or a planet occupying each part is placed in the divisional chart according to certain fixed rules.

Calculation of Divisional Charts

Some of the commonly used divisional charts are explained here.

Drekkana (D3)

Each rashi is divided into three parts of 10 degrees each, known as Drekkana. The first Drekkana belongs to the sign itself; the second Drekkana to the sign fifth from it and the third Drekkana to the ninth sign from it. This chart specifically pertains to one's siblings.

Saptamsha (D7)

Each sign is divided into seven equal parts of 4°17'8.5", called Saptamsha. In odd signs, the first Saptamsha belongs to the same sign; the remaining Saptamshas follow the same regular order. In even signs, the first Saptamsha belongs to the seventh sign from itself and the remaining Saptamshas follow the next signs in the same regular order. This chart is relevant to progeny.

Navamsha (D9)

Each sign is divided into nine equal divisions of 3°20' each, called Navamsha. The division of one Navamsha (3°20') is also equal to one pada (quarter) of a nakshatra. So this chart is according to the divisions of nakshatra padas. In moveable sign (1, 4, 7, 10), the first Navamsha belongs to the sign itself; in fixed signs (2, 5, 8, 11) the first Navamsha belongs to the ninth sign from itself; in dual signs (3, 6, 9, 12) the first Navamsha belongs to the fifth sign from itself. The remaining Navamshas follow the subsequent signs. Of all the usual divisional charts that astrologers employ for their routine predictions, the Navamsha is considered the most important. While this chart is to be analysed for all events in one's life, it specifically pertains to one's spouse.

Dashamsha (D10)

Each sign is divided into ten equal divisions of 3°00' each, called Dashamsha. The first Dashamsa in odd signs belongs to the sign itself and the subsequent Dashamshas follow the subsequent signs. The first Dashamsa in even signs belongs to the ninth sign from itself and the subsequent Dashamshas are placed in subsequent signs. This chart specifically pertains to the profession of the native.

Dwadashamsha (D12)

Each sign is divided into twelve equal divisions of 2°30' each, called Dwadashamsa. The first Dwadashamsa belongs

48

to the same sign, the next one to the subsequent sign, and so on. This divisional chart is particularly relevant to one's parents.

What to see from which Divisional Chart

Chart	Division	For	House	Significator
Drekkana	one-third (10°)	Younger brother-sister	third	Mars
		Elder brother-sister	eleventh	Jupiter
Saptamsha	one-seventh (4°17'8.5")	Children	fifth	Jupiter
Navamsha	one-ninth (3°20')	Spouse	seventh	Venus
Dashamsha	one-tenth (3°00')	Profession	tenth	Sun
Dwadashamsha	one-twelfth (2°30')	Mother	fourth	Moon
		Father	ninth	Sun

How to Analyse Divisional Charts?

Divisional charts are to be analysed in the same manner as the birth chart, independently and conjointly with the birth chart. In a general sense, a divisional chart may be employed to determine all about the native that is determined from the birth chart. In a specific sense, the relevant divisional chart should be referred to in order to know about a particular aspect of life or relation.

The strength of a particular house, house lord and karaka (significator) should be evaluated first in the birth chart. Then the relevant divisional chart should be analysed from the following six angles:

(a) Lagna and lagna lord of divisional chart

(b) Significator house and the house lord from the lagna.

For example in Dwadashamsha chart analyse fourth house for mother, ninth house for father.

(c) Treat the significator house as the lagna and analyse the chart. For example treat fourth house as the lagna in the Dwadashamsha chart and analyse the chart for mother.

(d) Analyse the strength of the natural significator and malefic and benefic influences on it.

(e) Also analyse the relevant house and condition of house lord treating natural significator as the lagna. For example treat the Moon as the lagna in the Dwadashamsha chart and analyse the fourth house for mother accordingly.

(f) Synthesise all this with the condition of relevant house lord of the birth chart in the divisional chart.

Note

Special importance of the lagna in a divisional chart lies in the fact that it generally represents its relevant house in the birth chart. Thus the Navamsha lagna represents the seventh house of the birth chart or spouse, the Drekkana lagna represents the third house or siblings, the Saptamsha lagna represents the fifth house or children and the Dashamsha lagna represents the tenth house or profession. The Dwadashamsha lagna similarly represents both the parents. When it comes to further specifics, then relevant houses of the divisional chart must also be taken into account. Thus, in the Drekkana chart, the third house represents the younger sibling while the eleventh house represents the elder sibling. Similarly, in the Dwadashamsha chart, the fourth house represents the mother while the ninth house represents the father.

A practical application of the divisional charts finds mention in chapters Ten and Eleven.

CHAPTER SIX

INTERPRETATION OF VIMSHOTTARI DASHA

Vedic System of Timing the Events

According to Maharshi Parashara there are forty-two types of dasha systems for timing the events in the life of a native. The most popular, time-tested and result-oriented dasha is the Vimshottari dasha. As the name suggests, the dasha span is of one hundred and twenty years.

Types of dashas

The dashas are broadly of two types:

(a) Planetary dashas

(b) Rashi dashas

Planetary Dashas

The total period of dasha system is divided in different parts and ruled by planets. The dasha operative at any time will be of a particular planet and the results will pertain to the natural signification, lordship, placement and strength of the planet. This will be termed as the mahadasha (MD) or the major period. The major period is further divided into antardashas (AD's) or sub-periods, normally according to the proportions of the major period. So in the major period of a planet, sub-periods of all the planets will come. The result of the major period and the sub-period will depend upon the mutual relationship of the major period lord and sub-period lord, their disposition in the birth chart and divisional charts, their lordship and their strengths. Some of the planetary dashas are: Vimshottari, Ashtottari, Shodashottari, Yogini, etc. Each AD or sub-period can be further divided into pratyantardashas (PD's) or sub-sub-periods. Further finer divisions called sookshma dasha and prana dasha can be resorted to for very close timing of events provided the birth time has been very accurately recorded.

Rashi Dashas

In these dashas the periods are ruled by different rashis (signs) instead of planets. In certain dashas the periods of the rashis are fixed and in some, the periods of the rashis are variable depending on certain conditions in the horoscope. The rashi dashas are further divided in sub-periods. So in the mahadasha (MD) of one rashi antardashas (AD's) or sub-periods of other rashis operate. Some of the rashi dashas are: Chara dasha, Sthira dasha, Kaala Chakra dasha, Kendradi dasha, etc.

Applicability

For Vimshottari, Yogini and some other dashas there is no condition of applicability to a horoscope while for some of the other dashas, Parashara has specified conditional applicability. For example:

- *Shodashottari dasha* (116 years): For births in *shukla paksha* and lagna in the Sun's Hora, and for birth in *krishna paksha* and lagna in the Moon's Hora, this dasha is applicable.

- *Dwadashottari dasha* (112 years): Gives fruitful results if birth lagna is in the Navamsha of Venus.

- *Ashtottari dasha* (108 years): Except lagna, Rahu in a kendra or a trikona from the lagna lord, Ashtottari dasha may be applied. Birth during day time in *krishna paksha* and birth in night during *shukla paksha*, Ashtottari dasha gives results.

- *Panchottari dasha* (105 years): Birth in Cancer lagna and in Dwadashamsha of Cancer (lagna should be less than 2°30' in Cancer), only Panchottari dasha gives results.

- *Shatabdika dasha* (100 years): Vargottama birth lagna (lagna in the same rashi in Navamsha as in birth chart), Shatabdika dasha is applicable.

- *Chatursheetisama dasha* (84 years): When tenth lord is in the tenth house in birth chart, Chatursheetisama dasha gives results.

- *Dwisaptatisama dasha* (72 years): When the lagna lord is in seventh house or the seventh lord in lagna, Dwisaptatisama dasha should be tried.

- *Shashtisama dasha* (60 years): When the Sun is in lagna, Shashtisama dasha should be applied.

- *Shatatrimshatsama dasha* (36 years): This dasha is applicable for birth during day and in Sun's Hora, or birth during night and in Moon's Hora. This dasha is similar to the Yogini dasha as for as the dasha duration of dasha lords is concerned but is different in that the lords of different dashas are different and not like the eight Yoginis of the Yogini dasha.

Structure of Vimshottari Dasha

The word Vimshottari literally means one hundred and twenty, so this dasha consists of a cycle of 120 years. This cycle of one hundred and twenty years is divided into nine parts ruled by the nine planets in order of the lordship of nakshatras. The dasha period allotted to each planet is as follows:

Planet	Years allotted	Nakshatra
Ketu	7	Ashwini, Magha, Moola
Venus	20	Bharani, P. Phalguni, P. Ashadha
Sun	6	Krittika, U. Phalguni, U. Ashadha
Moon	10	Rohini, Hasta, Shravana
Mars	7	Mrigshira, Chitra, Dhanishtha
Rahu	18	Ardra, Swati, Shatabhisha
Jupiter	16	Punarvasu, Vishakha, P. Bhadrapada
Saturn	19	Pushya, Anuradha, U. Bhadrapada
Mercury	17	Ashlesha, Jyeshtha, Revati

Total Period: 120 years

Calculation of Vimshottari Dasha

The dasha a native gets at the time of birth depends on the nakshatra occupied by the Moon in the birth chart. The first dasha operative at the time of birth is that of the lord of the Moon's nakshatra. Span of one nakshatra represent the total period ruled by its lord. The degrees traversed by the Moon in its nakshatra is the proportional period passed before the birth and the remaining degrees to be covered by the Moon is the balance of proportional dasha to be spent by the native at the time of birth.

For example if Moon is in Aries at 23°20', it is in Bharani nakshatra, ruled by Venus. As the Bharani nakshatra starts at 13°20' and ends at 26°40', the Moon at 23°20' has already covered 10 degrees and the remaining 3°20' are to be travelled. By proportional calculation, total period of dasha multiplied by the balance of degrees to be traversed by the Moon and divided by 13°20' gives the balance of dasha available to the native. So in this case:

$$\frac{\text{Period of nakshatra lord} \times \text{Balance of degrees to be covered by the Moon in the nakshatra}}{13°20'}$$

$$\frac{20 \text{ years of Venus} \times 3°20'}{13°20'} = 5 \text{ years balance of Venus}$$

The next dasha in the above case will be that of the Sun (6 years), then the Moon (10 years), Mars (7 years), etc. according to the order of the lords of the nakshatras.

Each major period is divided into nine sub-periods in proportion to the dasha periods of nine planets. The first sub-period starting in the major period is that of the planet whose major period is operative. For example the first sub-period in the major period of Mars will be that of Mars and then of Rahu, Jupiter, Saturn, etc., according to the order of the nakshatra lords. The reader may refer to general books on Vedic astrology for calculation of Vimshottari dasha.

Analysis of Vimshottari Dasha

Though there are many dasha systems, Maharshi Parashara has elaborated Vimshottari dasha the most. There are many principles given in the classics for the analysis of the Vimshottari dasha in detail while for some dashas only methods of calculation are given. Does it imply that other dashas need to be interpretted on the same guidelines as the Vimshottari dasha? It is for this reason that some basic principles of analysis of the Vimshottari dasha are compiled below.

A dasha lord gives results according to its lordship as well as other influencing factors, mainly:

(a) *Position* : a planet posited in a particular house will give results pertaining to that house.

(b) *Aspect* : a planet aspected by a particular planet will give results of the aspecting planet also.

(c) *Conjunction* : a planet conjoined with a particular planet will give effects of the conjoining planet also.

Dasha Results According to Planetary Strength

(1) If a planet is strong (see planetary strength in earlier chapter), its dasha gives health, wealth, prosperity, etc.

(2) If a planet is weak, its dasha gives loss of health, wealth, misery, etc.

(3) If a planet is proceeding towards its debilitation sign (*Avarohi*), its dasha gives troubles and difficulties.

(4) If a planet is proceeding towards its exaltation sign (*Aarohi*), its dasha proves auspicious.

(5) During the dasha of a planet possessing directional strength, the native will be successful in his ventures and will be benefitted from the direction indicated by the planet.

(6) If a planet in the divisional charts is in benefic signs (of Jupiter, Venus, Mercury, the Moon), its dasha proves beneficial.

Dasha Results According to Planetary Lordship

(1) The dasha of the lagna lord brings power, authority, wealth and general happiness to the native. It is the dasha of rise.

(2) The dasha of the lord of the second house gives trouble (second house is a killer house), but brings wealth to the native. It may prove bad for the spouse (eighth *from the seventh house*).

(3) The dasha of the lord of the third house reveals hidden talents of the native. It causes movement from the residence (twelfth *from the fourth house*) or short journeys.

(4) The dasha of the lord of the fourth house confers happiness, property, vehicles. This is generally a good

period. It may prove to be a bad period for the father (eighth *from the ninth house*).

(5) The dasha of the lord of the fifth house gives progeny, an inclination to study, wealth and *mantra siddhi*. Elder brother may also get married in this dasha as fifth house is seventh *from the eleventh house* of elder brother.

(6) The dasha of the sixth lord brings danger from enemies, diseases, accidents, debts, etc. In this dasha the native gains stamina to fight back the difficult times. This period arouses competitive tendencies in the native. This dasha is also favourable for the rise of father as it is tenth *from the ninth house*.

(7) In the dasha of the seventh lord, if eligible, the native gets married or forms new associations. Native becomes prominent in public, gets position or rise. The dasha proves favourable for business partnerships. This being the dasha of the killer house, danger to life is also present.

(8) The dasha of the lord of the eighth house may bring sudden danger, fear of death, sickness or even death. This dasha may also arouse past life habits or tendencies. Inclination towards spiritual or occult subjects becomes prominent. Tendency to become non-traditional or unorthodox becomes obvious. This dasha may drag the native into controversies and the hidden portion of one's life may get revealed as this house lies in the visible half of the zodiac. This dasha brings a change in the life pattern of the native. Eighth house being twelfth *from the ninth house*, its dasha may bring disgrace.

(9) During the dasha of the lord of the ninth house, the native performs acts of charity, religious duties, etc. He

visits religious places. It is generally a lucky period. This dasha may prove fatal for the co-borns (being seventh *from the third house*). Gain of progeny is also possible as it is fifth *from the fifth house*. It is also a period of sickness for the mother as it is sixth *from the fourth house* of mother.

(10) During the dasha of the lord of the tenth house, the native receives wealth, favours from the government. It is a period of professional excellence, rise and fame.

(11) During the dasha of the lord of the eleventh house, the income of the native increases. He gets achievements in his sphere of activity. In this dasha he may also get promotion in his job. This is a period of general gain. He may have children or his children may get married (being seventh *from the fifth house*). This is a period of accidents also (sixth *from the sixth house*) and is a bad period for mother (eighth *from the fourth house*).

(12) During the dasha of the twelfth lord, the native incurs much expenditure or invests money in different projects. Its dasha may give bed pleasures, confinement or even hospitalisation. The native may develop foreign connections.

Dasha Results According to Planetary Position

(1) If a planet is posited in a benefic house (kendra, trikona, etc.) its dasha will prove fruitful.

(2) If a planet is occupying any of the *Trik sthanas* (sixth, eighth or twelfth houses), its dasha will be harmful or evil producing.

(3) The dasha of a benefic planet proves malefic if it is in third, sixth or eleventh house or associated with their lords.

(4) The dasha of a malefic planet, if placed in the third, sixth or eleventh house, proves good.

(5) The most beneficial dasha is that of the lord of:
    (a) a kendra associated with trikona or trikona lord
    (b) a trikona associated with kendra or kendra lord

(6) The dasha of a planet aspected by the planets mentioned in (5) above also proves beneficial.

(7) The dasha of the lord of *Trik sthana* (sixth, eight or twelfth house) also becomes benefic if associated with a trikona lord.

(8) The dasha of a planet posited in a *maraka sthana* (second or seventh house) associated with *marakesha* (second or seventh lord), or in eighth house, proves fatal.

(9) A planet in first Drekkana (10°) gives result in the beginning of its dasha, in second Drekkana, in the middle of its dasha and in third Drekkana, at the end of its dasha. Reverse holds true for a retrograde planet.

Special Principles

(1) Treat the major period lord *as the lagna* and analyse the position of the sub-period lord with respect to the major period lord. For example if the sub-period lord is in the tenth from the major period lord – rise in profession; in fifth from the major period lord – results related to children, education, learning, etc. may occur.

(2) If the major period lord and sub-period lord are placed in kendra or trikona from each other, the period proves generally beneficial.

(3) If the major period lord and the sub-period lord are placed sixth-eighth (*shadashtaka*) to each other; or second-twelfth (*dwirdwadasha*) to each other, the period proves generally unfavourable.

(4) The dasha of the debilitated lord of the third, sixth or eighth house, or the dasha of the debilitated planet posited in the third, sixth or eighth house proves very good.

(5) The dasha of Rahu or Ketu gives the results of it's dispositor (they act as the lords of the signs where they are placed).

(6) Birth during Abhijit muhurta (mid point between sunrise and sunset, and between sunset and sunrise) proves auspicious. The Sun will be in the tenth or the fourth house in such cases.

CHAPTER SEVEN

THE MEANING IN PSYCHOLOGY OF YOGINIS

Every yogini clearly reveals the tendencies inherent in the personality of the individual whose horoscope is being read, in three ways:

(a) Through the literal meaning as revealed in the astro-logical classic, *Manasagari*.

(b) The modified meaning according to the relevant position occupied by the lord of the Yogini in a horoscope as explained in the instances given in this book.

(c) The other possibilities inherent, through the conjunction or aspects of other Yoginis on a particular Yogini as explained in the examples given in the book.

Results of the Yoginis in their Major Periods

Mangala (Moon): 1 year

This period causes inclination towards religion and pious or religious personages, devotion towards one's deity, provides all kinds of comforts, fame, riches, gain of conveyances from the ruler (government), gain of robes, jewellery, harmonious relations with the opposite sex, enhancement of knowledge, celebration of an auspicious event (marriage, etc.).

Pingala (Sun): 2 years

This period may give heart troubles, if indicated in the birth chart. This is a period of worries, mental and physical sufferings due to indulgence in the evil company, fruitless desires, immoral relationships, loss of wealth, fame and love. It may give blood diseases, fever and bilious pains. Suffering to children, servants, etc., and harm to good relations occurs.

Dhanya (Jupiter): 3 years

General features of this period are gain of wealth, comforts, prosperity in business, rise in fame, ruin of the enemies, gain of education, increase of knowledge, harmonious relations with the spouse. If eligible, it gives appreciation by the ruler (can be titles, decorations, etc., from the government). It creates opportunity for pilgrimages, and devotion to deities.

Bhramari (Mars): 4 years

This is the period of wanderings. It dislocates the person from his abode and he roams around for unproductive pursuits. A ruler loses his kingdom and is forced to wander here and there for his survival. For others, it can be a loss of position and then very hard work to regain the lost position.

Bhadrika (Mercury): 5 years

This period gives friendships, harmonious relations with the family members, religious or sacred persons and even with the rulers (people in high position in the government). In this period, an auspicious ceremony is held at home, availability of all kinds of comforts, keen interest in business activities. It also provides physical relations with the beautiful among the opposite sex.

Ulka (Saturn): 6 years

It gives loss of wealth, fame, vehicles, etc. This is a period of suffering to children, servants, etc. Loss from the government (in the form of penalty or fine, etc.), un-harmonious relations with the family members, ailments related to heart, stomach, ear, teeth, feet, etc., are the general features of this period.

Siddha (Venus): 7 years

It causes accomplishment of all pursuits, rise in good luck, fame, wealth, education, prosperity. It gives a post of authority by the government, inclination in the business, gain of wealth, robes, and jewels. Children may get married and one may get physical pleasures in this period.

Sankata (Rahu): 8 years

In this period, the native may experience loss of position, wealth, fire in the village, city and place of residence, fruitless desires, loss of minerals like gold, etc., separation from family, weakness of the body and the fear of death.

Results of the Yoginis in their Sub Periods

Sub periods in the major period of Mangala

Mangala-Managla (Moon-Moon): 10 days

Friendship circle grows, happiness regarding progeny, good physical health, harmonious relations with the spouse, celebrations at home.

Mangala-Pingala (Moon-Sun): 20 days

Bitter relations with the relatives, mental sorrow, many sufferings. Generally a bad period.

Mangala-Dhanya (Moon-Jupiter): 30 days (1 month)

Gains of vehicles, gains from children and friends, children may do well in this period, various kinds of comforts, luxuries, etc.

Mangala-Bhramari (*Moon-Mars*): 40 days (1 month 10 days)

Lack of harmonious relations with the opposite sex, stay in a foreign country, loss of wealth, and one gets introduced to a person placed at high places in the government.

Mangala-Bhadrika (*Moon-Mercury*): 50 days (1 mth 20 days)

Gain of wealth, grains, good relations with the spouse and the children, entertainment with friends and relatives, devotion to Gods.

Mangala-Ulka (*Moon-Saturn*): 60 days (2 months)

Loss of money and sufferings to children, spouse, friends, etc.; punishment from the government.

Mangala-Siddha (*Moon-Venus*): 70 days (2 months 10 days)

Happiness from the children and spouse, gain of money, comforts and luxuries, enjoyment of good relations with friends and relatives.

Mangala-Sankata (*Moon-Rahu*): 80 days (2 months 20 days)

Fear from fire, water, thieves, punishment from the government, death-like sufferings.

Sub periods in the major period of Pingala

Pingala-Pingala (*Sun-Sun*): 40 days (1 month 10 days)

Diseases, sorrows, sufferings from evil-habits, mental sufferings, depression, tension, etc.

Pingala-Dhanya (*Sun-Jupiter*): 60 days (2 months)

Gain of wealth, grains, progeny, comforts, luxuries, fulfilment of desires, and enjoyment from the opposite sex.

Pingala-Bhramari (*Sun-Mars*): 80 days (2 months 20 days)

Stay in a foreign country or place, losses in a place where one stays, loss from relatives, conflict among family members and relatives.

64

Pingala-Bhadrika (Sun-Mercury): 100 days (3 mths 10 days)

Gains from children (good period for children), rise of fame, prosperity in business, gains and benefits occur especially by change of place.

Pingala-Ulka (Sun-Saturn): 120 days (4 months)

Bitter relations with relatives and friends, punishment from the government, fear of theft, sorrow due to society, friends and acquaintances.

Pingala-Siddha (Sun-Venus): 140 days (4 months 20 days)

A period of gain from 'Mantras and Yantras', gain of wealth, grains, breathing troubles, diabetes.

Pingala-Sankata (Sun-Rahu): 160 days (5 months 10 days)

Loss of money, fear of disease, enemies, fear of punishment from the government.

Pingala-Mangala (Sun-Moon): 20 days

Ill-health, sorrows and sufferings due to attachments, loss of longevity.

Sub periods in the major period of Dhanya

Dhanya-Dhanya (Jupiter-Jupiter): 90 days (3 months)

Gains of lands and properties, wealth, grains, financial gains from the government, happiness from the children and the spouse.

Dhanya-Bhramari (Jupiter-Mars): 120 days (4 months)

Sorrows, wanderings, loss of wealth, difference of opinion with friends, etc. It indicates movement or takes one away from home (place of stay).

Dhanya-Bhadrika (Jupiter-Mercury): 150 days (5 months)

Good luck, happiness from friends and family members, increase of grains, attainment of a of dignified post (Prime

Ministership, etc.) gain of conveyances from the government, gain of property, good clothes, etc.

Dhanya-Ulka (*Jupiter-Saturn*): 180 days (6 months)

Various troubles, pain in the heart or waist, loss of wealth.

Dhanya-Siddha (*Jupiter-Venus*): 210 days (7 months)

Happiness from the children, meeting friends, various comforts and luxuries.

Dhanya-Sankata (*Jupiter-Rahu*): 240 days (8 months)

Imprisonment or confinement, lack of interest or inspiration in the work, business, etc.

Dhanya-Mangala (*Jupiter-Moon*): 30 days (1 month)

Occurrence of auspicious activities, comforts from wealth, jewellery, minerals, happiness from the spouse, children, etc.

Dhanya-Pingala (*Jupiter-Sun*): 60 days (2 months)

Loss of wealth, property, mental agony and dejection, fear from the government, headaches.

Sub periods in the major period of Bhramari

Bhramari-Bhramari (*Mars-Mars*): 160 days (5 mths 10 days)

Fear, pain and sufferings due to attachments, troubles from poisons (food poisoning, etc.) Sorrows from own people and the enemies too.

Bhramari-Bhadrika (*Mars-Mercury*): 200 days (6 mths 20 d)

Foreign travel, company of friends, gain of education, respect from the ruler (it can be an achievement of titles and decorations from the government).

Bhramari-Ulka (*Mars-Saturn*): 240 days (8 months)

Fever, pains, blood-impurity, sufferings to the spouse and the children, and monetary losses.

Bhramari-Siddha (*Mars-Venus*): 280 days (9 months 10 days)

Fulfilment of desires, gain of knowledge, wisdom, wealth, elimination of fears and diseases.

Bhramari-Sankata (*Mars-Rahu*): 320 days (10 mths 20 days)

Sorrows, sufferings due to attachments, wanderings, diseases (ill-health), fear of being named in the case of theft, loss of honour.

Bhramari-Mangala (*Mars-Moon*): 40 days (1 mths 10 days)

A good period, gains, comforts, benefits by serving the ruler (government).

Bhramari-Pingala (*Mars-Sun*): 80 days (2 mths 20 days)

Fear from the government, diseases of rectum, feet, mouth, etc.

Bhramari-Dhanya (*Mars-Jupiter*): 120 days (4 months)

Increase of wealth, gains of vehicles, enhancement of comforts and luxuries, defeat of enemies, good and harmonious relations with the government.

Sub periods in the major period of Bhadrika

Bhadrika-Bhadrika (*Mercury-Mercury*): 250 days (8m 10d)

Fame, goodwill, gain of conveyances, wealth, relief from bad habits and pains, knowledge of the divine-path.

Bhadrika-Ulka (*Mercury-Saturn*): 300 days (10 months)

Conflict with the people, ill health, loss at the place of stay (can be by theft, breakage, etc.) loss of wealth, mental sorrows.

Bhadrika-Siddha (*Mercury-Venus*): 350 days (11 mths 20d)

Devotion to gods and sacred personages, celebrations at home, enjoyments with family members and friends.

Bhadrika-Sankata (*Mercury-Rahu*): 400 days (1y 1m 10d)
Troubles, pains, sorrows, mental confusions, sufferings due to foreign travel.

Bhadrika-Mangala (*Mercury-Moon*): 50 days (1m 20d)
Fame, riches, lands, gains in the business, happiness from children, and addition to family (may be birth of a child in the family).

Bhadrika-Pingala (*Mercury-Sun*): 100 days (3 mths 10 days)
Gains from agriculture and property, gains occur specially by taking advice of the elder, bilious complaints.

Bhadrika-Dhanya (*Mercury-Jupiter*): 150 days (5 months)
Happiness from the children, spouse, friends, etc., entertainments, enjoyments and celebrations at home.

Bhadrika-Bhramari (*Mercury-Mars*): 200 days (6m 20 days)
Fear from fire or electricity, fear of death, loss of land and property, blood-impurity. It also gives happiness from one's own people.

Sub periods in the major period of Ulka

Ulka-Ulka (*Saturn-Saturn*): 360 days (1 year)
Sudden development of fear from enemies, losses, sorrows, loss of position, status, etc.

Ulka-Siddha (*Saturn-Venus*): 420 days (1 year 2 months)
Same malefic results as in case of Ulka-Ulka. In addition to the above, it gives foreign travels.

Ulka-Sankata (*Saturn-Rahu*): 480 days (1 year 4 months)
Fear of death, sufferings to the spouse, children, servants, friends, etc., danger to a family member.

Ulka-Mangala (*Saturn-Moon*): 60 days (2 months)
Attachments, happiness from friends, spouse, etc., gain of wisdom, wealth, relief from disease.

Ulka-Pingala (Saturn-Sun): 120 days (4 months)

Wanderings or travels, skin diseases and diseases of the head.

Ulka-Dhanya (Saturn-Jupiter): 180 days (6 months)

It is a 'no loss - no gain period'. It may give diseases of wind and cough. Conflicts with family members and friends.

Ulka-Bhramari (Saturn-Mars): 240 days (8 months)

Mental sorrows, confusions, fear of enemies, conflicts, etc.

Ulka-Bhadrika (Saturn-Mercury): 300 days (10 months)

General well-being, gain of wealth, but loss of good clothes and jewels, happiness from friends and relatives.

Sub periods in the major period of Siddha

Siddha-Siddha (Venus-Venus): 490 days (1y 4m 10 days)

Accomplishment of all objectives and desires, happiness from children and family members.

Siddha-Sankata (Venus-Rahu): 560 days (1y 6m 20d)

Confinement, loss of wealth by theft or by way of punishment by the ruler.

Siddha-Mangala (Venus-Moon): 70 days (2 months 10 days)

Comforts, luxuries, happiness from one's own people, gain of wealth from the government, fulfilment of all desires.

Siddha-Pingala (Venus-Sun): 140 days (4 months 20 days)

Development of an arrogant attitude, fear from fire, enmity with own people, accrual of illegal income, or income which is of others in a moral sense.

Siddha-Dhanya (Venus-Jupiter): 210 days (7 months)

Time to get benefitted from the good deeds done in the past life, fulfilment of all desires, accomplishment without much effort. A very lucky period.

Siddha-Bhramari (*Venus-Mars*): 280 days (9 months 10 days)
Uneasy displacement or movement from the place where one stays or is staying presently, travels, fear from the government, getting into bad habits.

Siddha-Bhadrika (*Venus-Mercury*): 350 days (11 mth 20 days)
Auspicious celebrations at home, comforts and luxuries, gain of education, development of good habits and good conduct, fulfilment of desires.

Siddha-Ulka (*Venus-Saturn*): 420 days (1 year 2 months)
Loss of wealth and food grains, suffering, sorrows, misfortunes, diseases of the rectum, and painful attachments.

Sub periods in the major period of Sankata

Sankata-Sankata (*Rahu-Rahu*): 640 days (1 yr 9 mth 10 days)
Death, punishment by the ruler or government, exile, monetary loss.

Sankata-Mangala (*Rahu-Moon*): 80 days (2 months 20 days)
Diseases of the head or other diseases, ill health, bad habits, suffering to the wife.

Sankata-Pingala (*Rahu-Sun*): 160 days (5 months 10 days)
Sudden financial loss, sorrow related to the children, fear from enemies.

Sankata-Dhanya (*Rahu-Jupiter*): 240 days (8 months)
Pains in the stomach, happiness from children, fame and popularity in one's own country and also in other countries.

Sankata-Bhramari (*Rahu-Mars*): 320 days (10 mths 20 days)
Wanderings to different places, loss to the house, city, town or country of the native, fear from enemies.

Sankata-Bhadrika (*Rahu-Mercury*): 400 days (1y 1m 10d)
Gain of education, jewels, clothes. Rise in fame and conflict with the enemies.

Sankata-Ulka (Rahu-Saturn): 480 days (1 year 4 months)

Loss of accumulated money, death or death-like circumstances, loss of conveyances, etc.

Sankata-Siddha (Rahu-Venus): 560 days (1y 6m 20d)

Varied encouragements, gain of physical health, general comforts, happiness from children, steady mental state.

The table below gives at a glance the nature of sub periods operating under various Yogini major periods (based on *Shri Ranbir Jyotirmahanibandh*).

Nature of various sub periods under the Yogini major periods

Major Period	Sub period		
	Benefic	Malefic	Neutral
1. Mangala	Mangala, Dhanya Bhadrika, Siddha	Pingala, Bhramari, Ulka, Sankata	—
2. Pingala	Mangala, Pingala, Dhanya, Bhadrika	Bhramari, Ulka, Sankata	Siddha
3. Dhanya	Mangala, Dhanya, Bhadrika, Siddha	Pingala, Bhramari, Ulka, Sankata	—
4. Bhramari	Mangala, Dhanya, Siddha	Pingala, Bhramari, Ulka, Sankata	Bhadrika
5. Bhadrika	Mangala, Pingala Dhanya, Bhadrika, Siddha	Ulka, Sankata	Bhramari
6. Ulka	—	Pingala, Dhanya, Bhramari, Bhadrika, Ulka, Siddha, Sankata	Mangala
7. Siddha	Mangala, Dhanya, Bhadrika, Siddha	Pingala, Bhramari, Ulka, Sankata	—
8. Sankata	Siddha	Mangala, Pingala, Dhanya, Bhramari, Ulka, Sankata	Bhadrika

CHAPTER EIGHT

QUICK USE OF YOGINI DASHA

It is well known that India's expert astrologers use more than one dasha to make sound predictions. Many Indian astrologers are able to give fastest predictions to their clients with whose problems they are familiar, by a quick use of Yogini dasha only. Such a quick use of Yogini dasha can be done by an astrologer with an old familiar horoscope of an old familiar client. Here even the Vimshottari dasha can be overlooked.

Anyone using Yogini dasha should try the method given here, occasionally, not commonly, not regularly. Ten such instances of snap-shot method are being given here.

Exercise

(a) Take the bare birth chart without the degrees of any planet except the Moon.

(b) Calculate the Yogini Dasha.

(c) Examine the present major and sub-period of the Yogini dasha running.

(d) Examine the lordship of the Yoginis.

(e) Examine the placement of the lords of Yoginis in the horoscope.

(f) Now, draw your own conclusions.

72

Case Study 1 :
Success in a competitive examination

Here the question was, whether the native, a young girl would be able to succeed in an examination to qualify for the selection for a medical course in the U.S.A.

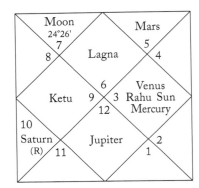

Jupiter			Venus Rahu Sun Mercury
Saturn (R)	Chart - 1		Mars
Ketu		Moon 24°26'	Lagna

She was running the major period of Sankata (Rahu) placed in the tenth house, the most powerful kendra. Rahu's dispositor Mercury is placed in own house. The sub-period was of Ulka (Saturn). Saturn is placed in the fifth house of education, an auspicious trikona house. It showed an achievement in education. She was selected as predicted.

Note: Before actually giving the prediction to her, the event was examined in detail in many other ways. This illustration is being given only to show that Yogini dasha can be employed for a quick prediction.

Case Study 2 :
Marriage of a girl

She had given her horoscope to us many years after her marriage, and the event of her marriage was examined retrospectively.

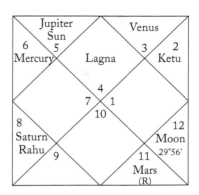

She was married in Dhanya-Dhanya. Jupiter, the lord of Dhanya, is in the second house aspected by the seventh lord Saturn from the fifth house of emotions.

Note: From Venus, the significator for marriage, Jupiter (Dhanya) is the seventh lord, aspecting the seventh house of marriage.

Case Study 3 :
Birth of a child

A prediction was earlier given to him about the birth of a child by employing other dashas. The Yogini dasha is tried now.

He was running major period of lagna lord Siddha (Venus), the lagna lord, in the sixth house and sub-period of Ulka (Saturn) aspecting the fifth house of children. Saturn

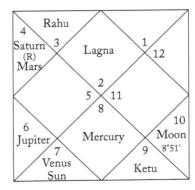

(Ulka) is also the ninth lord, which is an alternative house of children, being fifth *from fifth house*. Saturn (Ulka) also happens to be the lord of the fifth house from the major period of Siddha (Venus).

Note: *From Jupiter*, the significator for children, in Virgo, Venus (Siddha) is the ninth lord and Saturn (Ulka) is the fifth lord.

Case Study 4 :
Authorship

In this case, the person being an astrologer himself, had foreseen his forthcoming foreign trip.

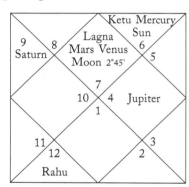

He was running Siddha (Venus) which being the lagna lord is auspicious and being conjoined with the tenth lord promises recognition of merit. The sub-period was Bhadrika (Mercury), the twelfth lord exalted in the twelfth house. No wonder, he got a prestigious invitation to address an international Vedic Astrology symposium in U.S.A.

Note: Mercury in Virgo promises authorship. During Siddha-Bhadrika, he produced as many as five books. Now, with the outset of Sankata (Rahu) since January 1995, the native has picked up enmity with several of his well-wishers. Having lost a lot of prestige, the Sankata dasha ensured he was never invited to USA again.

Case Study 5 :
Suicide by a disappointed artist

He came to know about his future in the field of music. He was very agitated and frustrated due to non-fulfilment of his ambition. A period of turmoil was foreseen and careful precautionary advice was also given to him. He could not withstand the mental turmoil and depression. He committed suicide in this period.

Ketu	Saturn Jupiter		
	Chart - 5		Moon 2°49'
			Lagna Venus
	Mercury	Sun	Mars Rahu

He was running Ulka-Pingala (Saturn-Sun) at that time. Saturn (Ulka) is the sixth lord of accidents and the seventh lord (killer). It is also debilitated, placed with eighth lord of sudden happenings and the fifth lord of emotions, Jupiter.

Sun (Pingala) is the lagna lord, debilitated and aspected by its enemy Saturn.

Note: Jupiter, the lord of the eighth house of life span, is afflicted by Saturn, Mars and the Sun.

Case Study 6 :
Tragic death of mother

A lady of Delhi gave her horoscope to us to know about her future prospects but the tragic death of her mother which occurred a few years ago was noticed and the event was traced in many ways. Here only Yogini dasha is discussed.

76

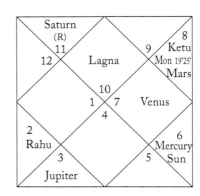

At the time of her mother's death she was running the major period of Mangala (Moon) and sub-period of Sankata (Rahu).

The Moon, the significator (karaka) for mother, is debilitated and is with Mars, lord of fourth house (mother). The Moon is also aspected by Saturn. The affliction is intensified as the Moon is in Rahu-Ketu axis.

From the Moon, Rahu is in the seventh house (killer), and the fourth lord Saturn is aspected by the sixth lord of disease, Mars.

It was due to such a severe affliction of the Moon and the fourth lord that her mother died of gut cancer during this period.

Case Study 7 :
A lucky period

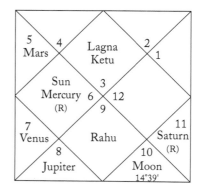

A prediction was given to this person by employing many dashas that he would get high elevation in his professional life.

He was running Ulka (Saturn), the ninth lord of good fortune, in the ninth house, and sub-period of Dhanya (Jupiter), the tenth lord of profession placed in the sixth house, aspecting the tenth house.

Note: From Saturn (Ulka), the major dasha lord, the sub-period lord Jupiter (Dhanya) is again in the tenth house of profession.

Case Study 8 :
Theft at business premises

In this case, the event was analysed retrospectively from many angles and many dasha systems. From Yogini dasha point of view, the analysis is given here.

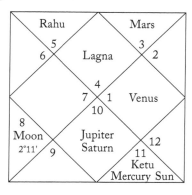

He was running the major period of Pingala (Sun), which is the lord of second house (money or valuables), placed in the eighth house of loss. The sub-period was of Bhadrika (Mercury) which is the twelfth lord of expenses or losses, placed with the second lord, the Sun, in the eighth house.

During this period some computers were stolen from his business premises and could not be recovered despite police intervention.

Case Study 9 : Cancer

A man while lying in the bed, after he was operated for cancer of rectum, wanted to know about his chances of survival. Why he had this painful surgical experience, in this particular period, was analysed.

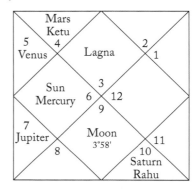

			Lagna
			Mars Ketu
Saturn (R) Rahu		Chart - 9	Venus
Moon 3°58'		Jupiter	Sun Mercury

At the time of the operation, the native was running the major and sub-period of Dhanya (Jupiter).

Jupiter, the seventh lord (killer), gives painful experience in its period, if not death. Jupiter is placed in the fifth house, aspected by the sixth lord of disease and debilitated Mars, (the planet of violence or surgery, alternatively). Saturn, the eighth lord (of serious or debilitating or incurable illness) too aspects this Jupiter from the eighth house.

Note: (a) *From the Moon*, Jupiter is the lagna lord placed in the eleventh house, an alternative house of disease (sixth *from sixth house*). Jupiter (Dhanya) is aspected by debilitated and afflicted Mars (lord of twelfth house of hospitalization), and Saturn, the second lord, a qualified killer.

(b) Saturn's aspect on the seventh lord Jupiter ensures a lingering disease of the body part represented by the seventh lord.

(c) The strength of exalted lagna lord is to be seen to be convinced that the native is still alive.

Case Study 10 :
Change in Job

A computer professional who asked for his future prospects was told that, after leaving the present job, he would get a better one.

Saturn (R)	Rahu	Moon 20°54'	
			Jupiter
	Chart 10		Lagna Sun Mercury Ven (R)
		Mars Ketu	

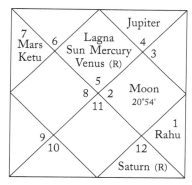

The native was running the major period of Ulka (Saturn). Saturn is the sixth and seventh lord placed in the eighth house, aspecting the tenth house. Saturn placed in the eighth house (change) has a potential to cause break or change in the present pattern.

The sub-period was of Sankata (Rahu), who is placed in the ninth house. The aspects of ninth lord Mars on its own house, and Rahu and tenth house, proved lucky for him. He resigned and joined a better computer organisation.

Note: (a) The sixth lord's placement in the eighth house is a classical Parashari Rajayoga called *Vipareeta Rajayoga*. It is a favourable yoga for betterment.

(b) The case was analysed by considering the concerned divisional chart and other dasha systems also.

Caution: The method shown in this chapter, should be used only in the case of familiar horoscopes and not on strangers' horoscopes.

Summary of the Events

Case	Event	Yogini Dasha	Relationship
1.	Success in a competitive examination	Sankata-Ulka (Rahu-Saturn)	Rahu - 10th house Saturn - 5th house
2.	Marriage	Siddha-Pingala (Venus-Sun)	Venus - Marriage lord in 12th house. The Sun - aspected by the 7th lord
3.	Birth of a child	Siddha-Ulka (Venus-Saturn)	Venus - 5th lord from the Moon Saturn - aspects 5th house
4.	Foreign Travel and Authorship	Siddha-Bhadrika (Venus-Mercury)	Venus - with 10th lord Mercury - signification for authorship
5.	Suicide	Ulka-Pingala (Saturn-Sun)	Saturn - 6th and 7th lord is debilitated and aspects the Sun, also debilitated. Lagna lord is aspected by 6th and 8th lord
6.	Mother died of Cancer	Mangala-Sankata (Moon-Rahu)	Moon - significator of the mother Rahu - Moon in Rahu-Ketu axis, debilitated and afflicted
7.	Lucky Period	Ulka-Dhanya (Saturn-Jupiter)	Saturn - 9th lord Jupiter - 10th lord
8.	Theft	Pingala-Bhadrika (Sun-Mercury)	Sun - 2nd lord in the 8th house Mercury - 12th lord with 2nd lord in 8th house
9.	Operated for Cancer	Dhanya-Dhanya (Jupiter-Jupiter)	Jupiter - 7th lord the killer aspected by the 6th and 8th lords.
10.	Change of a job	Ulka-Sankata (Saturn-Rahu)	Saturn - 8th house Rahu's dispositor aspects 10th house

Checklist

1. Examine the name of Yogini(s), whose period is running.
2. Examine the lordship of the Yoginis.
3. Examine the placement of the lords of the Yoginis in the horoscope.
4. Examine the nature of the aspects, if any, on these lords.
5. Examine the conjunction if any, with these lords.
6. Synthesise all these.
7. Draw your conclusions.
8. Now take a snap-shot view.

CHAPTER NINE

CONFIRMATION OF AN EVENT

To confirm the timing of an event, Vedic astrologers use at least two dashas, generally Vimshottari and Yogini. Once an event is reflected in the birth chart by employing one dasha system, it must be confirmed by using another dasha system. This time-tested approach is a potent tool for an astrologer, who can always cross-check an event and give definite predictions.

Here we are employing both, the Yogini and the Vimshottari dashas, to confirm an event.

Case Study 1 :
Scholastic achievement

This is the birth chart of a lady, B.Tech. (Engineer), a Hindu Brahmin girl, who married outside her community. Her scholastic abilities are discussed here which won her

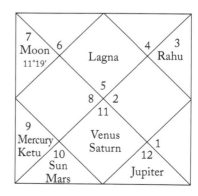

Jupiter			Rahu
Venus Saturn	**Chart - 1**		
Sun Mars			Lagna
Mercury Ketu		Moon 11°19'	

the UNDP (United Nations Development Project) Scholarship, which includes a brief training session in a foreign country.

Vimshottari Dasha : Jupiter-Rahu

The major period lord Jupiter is the fifth lord of education, aspecting the twelfth house of foreign country.

The sub-period was of Rahu, placed in the eleventh house of gains, aspecting the fifth house. The dispositor* of Rahu is Mercury, which is the second and the eleventh lord placed in the fifth house. An excellent money-making combination involving the house of education!

Yogini Dasha : Sankata-Sankata (Rahu-Rahu)

Rahu's role has already been discussed in getting her the scholarship. *From the Moon*, Rahu is in the ninth house of fortune, aspected by Mercury, the twelfth lord showing a foreign connection.

Note: A malefic planet placed in the eleventh house is praised by Parashara as being beneficial.

Case Study 2 :
Selection for marine engineering

This is the birth chart of a boy whose sister approached us to take advice about the career of her brother. He was to appear for an entrance examination for a course in marine engineering.

"Will he get selected?", was her query.

His horoscope is given on next page:

---

* The lord of the sign where a planet is posited is the dispositor of the planet posited in the sign. For example Rahu is in Gemini, whose lord is Mercury. Mercury is the dispositor of Rahu. According to Parashara, Rahu and Ketu give results as per their dispositors.

	Lagna Mars		Saturn (R) Ketu
		Chart - 2	
Venus (R) Sun Jup. Mercury			
Rahu		Moon 14°00'	

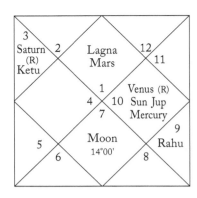

Vimshottari Dasha : Jupiter-Sun

Jupiter is the ninth lord of luck placed in the tenth house of distinction. Jupiter as twelfth lord placed in tenth house of profession takes the person away from home to discharge the duties of his profession. Jupiter as lord of Pisces, a watery sign, in the house of profession involves marine line.

The Sun is the lord of fifth house of intellect placed in the tenth house.

Note: (a) The combination of fifth or ninth (trikona houses) lord with any kendra (quadrant) lord is a Rajayoga.

(b) Sun in the tenth house has full directional strength.

Yogini Dasha : Ulka-Bhadrika (Saturn-Mercury)

Saturn (Ulka), the tenth lord and the eleventh lord is in the third house, placed with the technical planet, Ketu. Saturn aspects the fifth house of intellect and ninth house of luck. The tenth lord Saturn's aspect on Pisces shows profession related to marine life.

The sub-period was of Bhadrika (Mercury). Mercury is the sixth lord of competitions, placed in the tenth house of distinction. Mercury and Jupiter combination in the tenth house is a good combination for vidya (learning).

Note: Saturn and Mercury, the Yogini dasha lords, have exchanged their houses.

Case Study 3 :
Death of father in a vehicular accident

This girl was only thirteen years old when her father died in a vehicular accident. The horoscope was passed to us four year after the tragic event. The event is being analysed retrospectively.

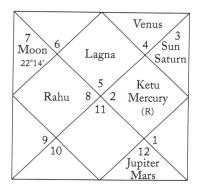

Jupiter Mars		Ketu Mercury (R)	Sun Saturn
			Venus
	Chart - 3		
			Lagna
	Rahu	Moon 22°14'	

See affliction to the significator of father, the Sun, and the ninth lord Mars.

(a) The ninth lord Mars is in the eighth house with the eighth lord Jupiter and is aspected by the sixth lord Saturn.

(b) *From the Moon*, the ninth lord Mercury is in the eighth house, afflicted by Rahu-Ketu axis.

(c) *From the Sun* (significator of father), the eighth and ninth lord Saturn is with the Sun, aspected by the sixth lord of accidents, Mars.

Vimshottari Dasha : Jupiter-Rahu

Jupiter, the eighth lord of sudden mishaps and obstructions is, with the ninth lord Mars.

The sub-period was of Rahu, placed in the fourth house (eighth *to the ninth house* of father). Mars, the dispositor of Rahu, is again the ninth lord placed in the eighth house.

Note: Mars is the fourth lord of vehicles aspected by the sixth lord of accidents, Saturn.

Yogini Dasha : Ulka-Siddha (Saturn-Venus)

Saturn (Ulka), the sixth lord of accidents, aspects the ninth lord Mars. The sub-period lord Venus (Ulka), the third lord of longevity of parents and significator of vehicles is in the twelfth house.

From the Sun (significator of the father), Saturn (Ulka) is the eighth and the ninth lord aspected by sixth lord Mars. Venus (Siddha) is in the second house from the Sun and, therefore, becomes killer for the father.

Case Study 4 :
Abduction

People have not forgotten the case of a tea estate manager in the eastern valley of India, who was kidnapped by terrorists, which led to many speculations and gossip. An astrological follow-up of the above case is given for our purpose of using the Yogini dasha.

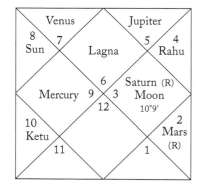

		Mars (R)	Saturn (R) Moon 10°9'
	Chart - 4		Rahu
Ketu			Jupiter
Mercury	Sun	Venus	Lagna

Vimshottari Dasha : Saturn-Jupiter

Saturn is the sixth lord of difficulties, placed in the tenth house of profession. The retrograde Saturn afflicts the Moon, responsible for the trauma this person had to undergo.

The sub-period was of Jupiter, the fourth lord of residence (the place where the native and his immediate family lives), and the seventh lord of *marakasthana* (killer house, often gives an agonising period) is placed in the twelfth house of captivity and is also aspected by the sixth lord Saturn. So a complete combination of mental and physical torture emerges, if the aspect of violent Mars (the eighth lord) on the sub-period lord Jupiter, the lagna lord Mercury, and the Sun, is also included.

Yogini Dasha : Bhadrika-Bhadrika (Mercury-Mercury)

The native was running both the major and the sub-period of Bhadrika (Mercury). Mercury is the lagna lord and the tenth lord of profession, placed in the fourth house. Mercury is aspected by the sixth lord Saturn which being retrograde expresses re-doubled fury.

Mercury is also aspected by the eighth lord of sudden and unforeseen dangers, a violent Mars, all the more dreaded here being retrograde. So the dasha lord Mercury is under double malefic influence of the sixth and the eighth lords.

Jupiter, the divine protector, is also aspecting Mercury. The person survived the incident.

Case Study 5 :
Marriage

Since childhood this girl used to stammer while speaking. She was given speech therapy, which proved of no use. Gradually it affected her confidence and an inferiority complex developed in her. She lost interest in her studies and had to abandon her schooling. Her marriage, in such circumstances, seemed a difficult proposition. The horoscope was analysed for timing her marriage. She got engaged within the predicted time frame. The horoscope was examined thoroughly by using the concerned

Rahu	Saturn (R)		
		Chart - 5	
			Mars Jupiter
	Moon 11°29'	Venus Mercury	Lagna Sun Ketu

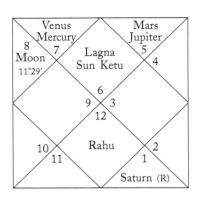

divisional charts but only Vimshottari and Yogini dashas are discussed here.

Vimshottari Dasha : Mercury-Saturn

Mercury is the lagna lord, placed with the marriage maker Venus, the ninth lord. *From the Moon*, Mercury is placed with the seventh lord of spouse, Venus.

The sub-period lord Saturn is aspected by the seventh lord Jupiter.

From the Moon, Saturn which is debilitated, is placed in the sixth house and aspected by the seventh lord Venus.

From Venus, Saturn is in the seventh house.

Note: If the sixth lord is debilitated or a debilitated planet is in the sixth house, the difficulties are eased out.

Yogini Dasha : Siddha-Sankata (Venus-Rahu)

Venus (Siddha) is a potential marriage giver and in this case is the lord of ninth house of luck. *From the Moon*, Venus (Siddha) is the seventh lord of life partner, placed in the twelfth house of bed comforts.

The sub-period was of Rahu (Sankata) placed in the seventh house. The dispositor of Rahu is Jupiter, who is again posited in the twelfth house.

From Venus, Rahu is in the sixth house, aspected by the seventh lord Mars.

Case Study 6 :
Tender is tough (Talent in sports)

Any person will take some time to digest the news which hit the newspapers of Delhi, "A thirteen year old boy trains commandos of Delhi Police". The boy achieved fame at national and international level. He also started earning money at quite an early age. A person knowing astrology will not be astonished at all, if he knows the horoscope.

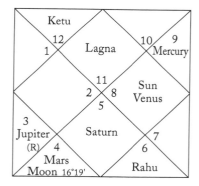

The horoscope is full of combinations of valour, fighting skill and earning money. A few of them are:

(a) The tenth lord of deeds in the sixth house of fight with the sixth lord, indicates the amount of fighting involved in his profession.

(b) The third lord Mars is debilitated in the sixth house, a combination praised by Maharshi Parashara.

(c) *From the Moon*, Rahu, a malefic in the third house of valour, is good for bravery, stamina and athletic skills.

(d) A very strong money producing combination – Jupiter, the second lord of money and the eleventh lord of gains is in the fifth house (*Lakshmi sthana*) and the fifth lord Mercury in the eleventh house (i.e., an exchange between the 5th lord and the 11th lord).

(e) The Sun is *digbali* (having directional strength) along with the ninth lord Venus.

Note: The third, sixth and tenth houses are for distinction in sports.

Vimshottari Dasha : Mercury-Rahu

Since childhood he has been running the major period of Mercury, the fifth lord of aptitude and the eighth lord of unforeseen dangers. Mercury is also the third and the twelfth lord from the Moon. During the major period of Mercury he visited many foreign countries for exhibition matches.

He obtained prominence in this field in the sub-period of Rahu, whose contribution has been explained in point (c) earlier.

Yogini Dasha : Ulka-Bhadrika (Saturn-Mercury)

He was running the major period of Ulka (Saturn). Saturn is the lagna lord and the twelfth lord of foreign influences, placed in the seventh house of public life. Saturn also aspects the ninth house of luck.

His work was noticed at national and international level, especially in the sub-period of Mercury (Bhadrika). The role of Mercury has already been discussed above.

Note: (a) *From the Moon*, Mercury, the twelfth lord is involved in an exchange with the sixth lord Jupiter, creating Scholarship Vipareeta rajayoga, a favourable combination for achievement in adversity. If you want to go deeper, search in the Dashamsha.

(b) *From the Moon*, Mercury the third lord is in sixth house and Rahu in third house. Mercury is in the house of honours. (A planet in the eleventh house promises honours).

Case Study 7 :
A pleasant surprise (Talent in acting)

Without having received any formal training, the inherent artistic talent of this girl was recognised suddenly. The concentration of four planets in the twelfth house aspected by Jupiter, clearly point towards recognition of such talents from far off places.

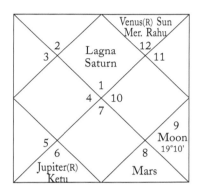

Venus(R) Sun Mer. Rahu	Lagna Saturn		
	Chart - 7		
Moon 19°10'	Mars		Jupiter (R) Ketu

Vimshottari Dasha : Moon-Mercury

She was selected for acting in a film in the major period of the Moon and the sub-period of Mercury. The Moon aspects the third house and Mercury is the third lord. Mercury being connected with Venus and Rahu led to her appearance in a foreign film, for which shooting was done outside India.

Yogini Dasha : Bhadrika-Siddha (Mercury-Venus)

She was running the major period of Bhadrika (Mercury). Mercury is the third lord but associated with Venus in the twelfth house. Sub-period was of Siddha (Venus). Venus again being in the twelfth house, brought her recognition, and being the second lord exalted in the twelfth house, shows money from foreign sources.

Note: The third house and third lord indicate talents, hobbies, etc.

Case Study 8 :
Fatality for Father

This is the horoscope of a person who lost his father in his 40th year. We are analysing this case to know the tragic period for his father, which should be reflected in the two dasha systems we are using.

Mercury (R) Sun	Jupiter		Moon 7°40'
Venus Rahu	**Chart - 8**		
			Lagna Ketu
		Mars (R)	Saturn (R)

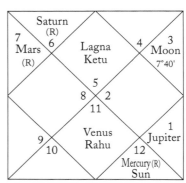

Vimshottari Dasha: Saturn-Venus

He was running the major and sub-periods of Saturn and Venus, respectively.

The major period lord Saturn is placed in the sixth house *from the ninth house* of father. Saturn also aspects the Sun, the significator for father.

From karaka the Sun, Saturn is placed in the seventh house, a *maraka* (killer) house for father.

The sub-period lord Venus is the third lord and denotes the longevity of the parents. Venus is also the third and eighth lord *from the Sun*, so it doubly represents the longevity of the father.

Note: Saturn and Venus are placed in *shadashtaka* (sixth-eighth) position from each other.

Yogini Dasha: Dhanya-Bhadrika (Jupiter-Mercury)

The native was running the Yogini dasha of Dhanya and sub-period of Bhadrika (Jupiter-Mercury).

The major period lord Jupiter, the eighth lord of fatality, placed in the ninth house of father, indicating danger to father.

The sub-period lord Mercury is placed with the Sun, the significator for father. Both are placed in the eighth house.

From karaka the Sun, Jupiter is in the second house, a *marakasthana* (killer house), and Mercury is the *marakesha* (killer lord) for father.

Case Study 9 :
Education in a foreign country

This is the horoscope of a boy who is a chemical engineer. He was selected for overseas education. Here we are analysing his selection by using two dasha systems.

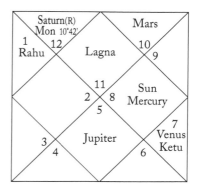

Vimshottari Dasha : Mercury-Jupiter

At the time of his selection, he was running the major period of Mercury and the sub-period of Jupiter. Mercury is the fifth lord of education placed in the tenth house of distinction.

The sub-period lord Jupiter is the fifth lord *from Mercury* placed in the tenth house of profession. Jupiter is aspected by an exalted tenth lord Mars from the twelfth house (overseas).

Note: (a) From the major period lord Mercury, the sub-period lord Jupiter is placed in the tenth house of profession.

   (b) Fifth house from Mercury also indicates higher education.

   (c) Placement of the fifth lord in the tenth house indicates education related to one's profession.

Yogini Dasha : Pingala-Bhadrika (Sun-Mercury).

The native was running Pingala-Bhadrika (Sun-Mercury).

Both the major period lord, the Sun, and sub-period lord, Mercury, are placed in the tenth house, indicating an excellent period of distinction in the field of education.

Case Study 10 :
Mishap during mountaineering expedition (Vehicular accident)

This is the case study of a mountain expedition, which was not even disrupted, but proved to be an unforgettable tragedy for some and a traumatic experience for many.

We are taking the horoscope of a person who was one among the team, who was heading for the destination, on September 15, 1981, without knowing the intentions of the destiny.

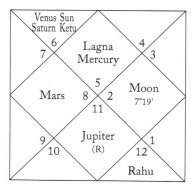

Vimshottari Dasha: Rahu-Venus

The native was running Rahu-Venus.

The major period lord Rahu is in the eighth house of sudden events. Rahu is aspecting the lagna lord, the Sun and the sixth lord of accidents, Saturn.

The sub-period was of Venus, the third lord of travelling, expedition, etc. Saturn, the sixth lord and the seventh lord (killer) is in close proximity (degree-wise) with the sub-period lord Venus.

An accident, during such a period, was inevitable.

Yogini Dasha : Bhadrika-Bhramari (Mercury-Mars)

The major period was of Bhadrika (Mercury), which is the eleventh lord (being sixth *from sixth* is an alternate house of accidents). Mercury is also the second lord (killer), aspected by the eighth lord, retrograde Jupiter.

Mars (Bhramari) is the fourth lord of vehicles and is aspected by the sixth lord of accidents, Saturn. The result being a vehicular accident.

The accident occurred in a most fierce way, as a military truck collided head on with the bus carrying the expedition team. Three or four people died, and many injured.

Protective aspect of Jupiter

Since Jupiter is aspecting the lagna from the seventh house and lagna lord, the Sun (by its retrograde aspect from previous house), the native was saved, but not without having suffered a fractured pelvis.

Note: Affliction to the Sun as the lagna lord gives fracture to the bones, as the Sun is the significator of bones.

Summary of the Events

Case Study	Event	Dasha	Relationship
1.	Scholastic Achievements	*Yogini* Sankata-Sankata (Rahu-Rahu)	Rahu in 11th house. Dispositor Mercury in 5th house.
		Vimshottari Jupiter-Rahu	Jupiter – the 5th lord aspects the 12th house. Rahu – in the 11th house, aspects the 5th house.
2.	Selection for a course in marine engineering	*Yogini* Ulka-Bhadrika (Saturn-Mercury)	Saturn – the tenth lord, aspects the 5th house. Mercury – in tenth house, with the 5th lord.
		Vimshottari Jupiter-Sun	Jupiter – in tenth house, with the 5th lord. Sun – the 5th lord, in the 10th house, with the 6th lord.
3.	Death of father in a vehicular accident	*Yogini* Ulka-Siddha (Saturn-Venus)	Saturn – the 6th lord aspects the 9th lord. Venus-in the 2nd house from the Sun.
		Vimshottari Jupiter-Rahu	Jupiter – the 8th lord with the 9th lord. Rahu – in the 6th house from the Sun.
4.	Abduction	*Yogini* Bhadrika-Bhadrika (Merc.-Merc.)	Mercury – Lagna lord, aspected by the 6th lord and the 8th lord.
		Vimshottari Saturn-Jupiter	Saturn – the 6th lord, aspects the lagna lord. Jupiter – the 4th lord in the 12th house.
5.	Marriage	*Yogini* Siddha-Sankata (Venus-Rahu)	Venus – natural marriage maker. Rahu – in the seventh house.
		Vimshottari Mercury-Saturn	Mercury – with Venus Saturn – aspected by the 7th lord.

Case Study	Event	Dasha	Relationship
6.	Tender is Tough [Talent in sports, fame and foreign travels]	*Yogini* Ulka-Bhadrika (Saturn-Mercury)	Saturn – the 12th lord aspects the 9th house. Mercury – 3rd and 12th lord from the Moon.
		Vimshottari Mercury-Rahu	Mercury – explained above. Rahu – in 3rd house from the Moon.
7.	A pleasant surprise [Talent in acting]	*Yogini* Bhadrika-Siddha (Mercury-Venus)	Mercury – the 3rd lord with Venus. Venus – represents artistic persuits.
		Vimshottari Moon-Mercury	Moon – aspects the 3rd house. Mercury – the 3rd lord with Venus.
8.	Fatality for father	*Yogini* Dhanya-Bhadrika (Jupiter-Mercury)	Jupiter – the 8th lord in the 9th house. Mercury – the 7th lord from the Sun.
		Vimshottari Saturn-Venus	Saturn – in the 7th house from the Sun. Venus – the 8th lord from the Sun.
9.	Education in a foreign country	*Yogini* Pingala-Bhadrika (Sun-Mercury)	Sun – with the 5th lord. Mercury – the 5th lord. Both are aspected by 12th lord retrograde Saturn.
		Vimshottari Mercury-Jupiter	Mercury – same as above. Jupiter – the 5th lord from Mercury.
10.	Mishap during mountaineering expedition. [Vehicular accident]	*Yogini* Bhadrika-Bhramari (Mercury-Mars)	Mercury – lord of killer house. Mars – the 4th lord aspected by the 6th lord.
		Vimshottari Rahu-Venus	Rahu – in 8th house Venus – with the 6th lord.

CHAPTER TEN

SUCCESSFUL PREDICTIVE TECHNIQUES

Successful prediction, though a rare feat, is the ultimate aim of any astrologer. Such predictions although spectacular, are always preceded by a thorough process of analysis. An intelligent use of two dasha systems is the back bone of any astrological technique to time an event and the study of the relevant divisional charts adds another dimension to the analysis.

Divisional charts have always played a vital role in clinching a brilliant prediction, provided an accurate birth time is known. While various Ayanamshas are being used by the different astrologers, we stick to Chitrapaksha Ayanamsha which is the most widely used Ayanamsha by Vedic astrologers the world over. This Aynamsha has given us the best results so far. Without going into the intricacies of the debate about the correctness of the Ayanamsha, we are simply using this Ayanamsha and showing the results, which serves our purpose very well.

How divisional charts are interpreted has already been discussed in chapter V.

In this chapter, we are revealing the classical approach of predicting brilliantly, by using the divisional charts. After going through all these cases, one is convinced about the soundness of this approach, as well as the great system the Vedic astrology is.

Case Study 1 :
Criminal Inclination (*use of Navamsha*)

Follow this case closely since we are now giving the full data along with the degrees of the planets. We are, however, not disclosing the identity of the person. This boy was running the Vimshottari dasha of Saturn, the eighth and the ninth lord placed in the third. The sub-period was of Jupiter, the seventh and the tenth lord placed in the lagna aspecting the ninth house. We can thus see both Saturn and Jupiter the major and sub-period lords aspecting the ninth house along with the sixth lord Mars. The ninth house thus receives the aspect of two malefic Saturn and

Ketu	Sun Mercury	Venus	Lagna Jupiter
	Case One Birth Chart		Mars Moon
			Saturn
			Rahu

Lagna	26°01'	Mars	20°00'	Venus	25°42'
Sun	28°30'	Mercury	2°36'	Saturn	0°22'
Moon	4°57'	Jupiter	11°45'	Rahu	11°07'

	Saturn Mercury Rahu	Lagna	
	Navamsha (D9)		
Mars Jupiter			Moon Venus
Sun		Ketu	

Mars. The sub-sub-period was of Venus who is the fifth lord from lagna placed in the twelfth house, which represents education in a far off place and also the jail. *From the Sun*, the significator for father, Venus happens to be the second and the seventh lord indicating a bad time for his father.

The father of the boy who has been earning fabulously in a foreign country was unhappy with the educational performance of this boy and scolded him. The boy talked about this with his young classmates in USA, who suggested that instead of his suffering such humiliation, he should get his father killed. Before the young Indian boy could react, the American boys contacted a killer gang. But another American boy decided to inform the FBI, which promptly got into action, chased the boy and collected substantial evidence. The boy was arrested, put inside the jail and is undergoing a criminal trial.

Criminal Psychology

This incident is now being explained astrologically. The tendencies which created such criminal feelings in the boy are seen thus:

(a) It is well known that the personality of an individual should be examined from the lagna. Here fortunately Jupiter is in the lagna while the lagna lord Mercury is in the eleventh house with exalted Sun.

(b) The psychology is largely determined by the Moon who, though in its own house in Cancer, is with violent sixth lord Mars, who is aspecting the ninth house of father.

(c) The mind or the intellect should be seen from the disposition of Mercury who is in the eleventh house in the nakshatra of Ketu and with exalted Sun.

(d) Along with all this, the fifth house from the lagna should also be examined. In this case the fifth house receives the aspects of Saturn (third aspect), Mars (fourth aspect), the Sun and Mercury (the seventh aspect) and Jupiter (the fifth aspect).

(e) The fifth lord Venus in the twelfth house receives the aspect of Saturn, who is both the eighth and the ninth lord.

Navamsha

(a) In the Navamsha, the lagna lord Venus is aspected by exalted Mars (the eighth aspect).

(b) The Moon also receives the aspect of exalted Mars.

(c) The fifth lord Mercury is in the twelfth house with two malefics Saturn, and Rahu and receives the aspect of exalted Mars again.

Note: Mars in the ninth house is aspecting the lagna lord, the Moon and the ninth lord from the ninth house.

Certain Combinations

The notable combinations here are:

(a) Afliction of the Moon, Mercury and fifth house and fifth lord. Afflictions of the Moon and Mercury are known to lead to mental aberrations.

(b) Malefic combinations involving the sixth and the eighth lords.

(c) Planets in sarpa drekkana (sarpa drekkanas are the second and third drekkanas of Karka – Cancer, the first and second dekkanas of Vrishchika - Scorpio, and the third of Meena – Pisces). Here Mars, the debilitated sixth lord, falls in the sarpa drekkana and afflicts the Moon and the fifth house.

(d) In the birth chart aspect of the eighth lord Saturn on the fifth lord Venus in the twelfth house is the major cause of the disturbance of studies of this boy.

The dasha unfolds the remaining part of the story.

Vimshottari Dasha

The boy was running the major period of Saturn, the eighth and the ninth lord, dangerously placed in *rashi gandanta* (the end or the beginning of a rashi). Here Saturn's degree is 0°22'.

The sub-period is that of Jupiter, whose ownership of the seventh and tenth houses brings into focus such plan which cannot be kept hidden. But in the Navamsha, Jupiter is not merely debilitated but also with Mars in the ninth house and aspected by Saturn from the twelfth house. The boy's hostile feelings towards his father led to his (the boy's) imprisonment. The sub-sub-period was that of Venus in the twelfth aspected by Saturn, showing interruption to education as already discussed.

Yogini Dasha

In Yogini it was major period of Ulka (Saturn). Thus we see that according to both the Vimshottari and the Yogini, Saturn becomes an effective cause for the evil tendencies of the boy. The sub-period was of Pingala (Sun), the third lord.

In the Yogini dasha Saturn in the third and the Sun as the owner of the third house added fuel to the fire when it came to rashness of the boy.

Saving Grace

Jupiter in the lagna aspecting the fifth and the ninth houses proved effective in stopping the boy from the commission of the contemplated crime.

In the navamsha, Jupiter from the ninth house aspects both the lagna and the fifth house. Through some spiritual merit of the past life (fifth house) the boy's father (ninth house) was saved.

Case Study 2 :

Period of Rise for Spouse (use of Navamsha)

Now in this horoscope we will show that Navamsha chart can be used to predict events pertaining to one's spouse.

The wife of this police officer contested the elections for the Lok Sabha (lower house of Parliament) and won.

Vimshottari Dasha

He was running the major period of Saturn and sub-period of Rahu.

Lagna		Moon	
Rahu	**Case Two**		
Saturn (R)	**Birth Chart**		Ketu Sun Mercury
		Venus Mars	Jupiter

North Indian diamond chart (Birth Chart):
- 2 Moon, 1, Lagna, 11, 10 Saturn (R), Rahu
- 12, 3, 9, 6
- Jupiter, 8
- 4, 5 Ketu Sun Mercury, 7 Venus Mars

Lagna	5°20'	Mars	17°47'
Sun	25°26'	Mercury	25°06'
Moon	22°00'	Jupiter	7°21'

Venus	2°16'
Saturn (R)	17°40'
Rahu	5°46'

Mars Jupiter		Ketu	Saturn
	Navamsha		Moon
	(D9)		
			Lagna
	Mercury Sun Rahu	Venus	

North Indian diamond chart (Navamsha D9):
- 7 Venus, 6, Lagna, 4, 3 Saturn, Moon
- Mercury Sun Rahu, 5, 8, 2 Ketu, 11
- 9, 10, 1, 12 Mars Jupiter

Birth Chart

Major period lord, Saturn is in the eleventh house (fifth house *from seventh*), the house of dignity for the spouse. Saturn is aspected by Jupiter, placed in the seventh house. Saturn is also aspected by Mars the ninth lord of luck.

From Venus (the significator for spouse), Saturn is the fifth lord of dignity placed in the fourth house of Parliament.

From the Lagna, the sub-period lord Rahu is placed in the twelfth house but is aspected by the seventh lord Mercury.

From Venus, Rahu is in the fifth house, aspected by the eleventh lord of gains, the Sun, representing government. Rahu is also aspected by the ninth lord of luck, Mercury.

Navamsha

Saturn as the seventh lord is in the eleventh house of gains aspected by Mars the fourth lord of Parliament.

Note: Saturn is also the seventh lord of public life. Rahu is in the fourth house, placed with the Royal planet Sun, aspected by the fifth lord Jupiter.

Yogini Dasha

He was running Yogini dasha of Bhadrika and sub-period of Sankata (Mercury-Rahu).

Birth Chart

Mercury (Bhadrika) is the seventh lord, placed in the royal sign Leo with the royal planet, Sun.

Note: Mercury, the seventh lord, placed in the sixth house of fight, represents elections in this case.

From Venus, Mercury is the ninth lord placed in the eleventh house of gains with the eleventh lord the Sun. It is a combination for favour from the government.

Rahu (Sankata) is also aspected by the seventh lord Mercury.

From Venus, Rahu (Sankata) is in the fifth house, aspected by the ninth lord Mercury, and the Sun, the government.

From the lagna, Saturn, the dispositor of Rahu, is in the eleventh house of gains aspected by Jupiter from the seventh house.

Navamsha

Mercury (Bhadriaka) and Rahu (Sankata) both are in the fourth house of parliament, with the Sun, aspected by Jupiter.

We notice that in this case Yogini Dasha is giving clearer indications as compared to the Vimshottari Dasha.

Case Study 3 :
An Accident (*use of Navamsha*)

He became the heart throb of millions of Indians. His popularity crossed the barriers of caste, creed and religion. Though he died many times on the silver screen, but now this was a dose too realistic for his fans. In July 1982, he met with an accident during the shooting of one of his films, and he was hanging between life and death, in the Beach Candy hospital of Bombay.

Vimshottari Dasha

At the time of the accident he was running Saturn-Sun.

Birth Chart

Saturn, the lagna lord, placed in the fourth house aspects the sixth house. The Sun is the seventh lord (killer) placed in the eighth house of sudden mishaps with the eighth lord Mercury, debilitated Venus and violent Mars.

From the Moon, Saturn is in the eighth house. The Sun is in the twelfth house of hospital, placed with the seventh lord (killer) Mars, and the eighth lord debilitated Venus. He was hospitalized and operated upon.

		Saturn (R)	
Lagna Ketu	**Case Three Birth Chart**		Jupiter
			Rahu
		Moon	Merc (R) Venus Sun Mars

Lagna	1°59'	Mars	22°36'	Venus	15°11'
Sun	24°23'	Mercury (R)	23°39'	Saturn (R)	19°14'
Moon	10°19'	Jupiter	0°32'	Rahu	10°32'

		Venus	Saturn
	Navamsha (D9)		Jupiter Mars Rahu
Moon Ketu			Sun Mercury
		Lagna	

Navamsha

Saturn aspects the sixth house of accidents. Saturn also aspects the sub-period lord Sun.

Note: Aspect of Saturn on the Sun is not good for vitality.

From the Moon, Saturn is in the sixth house and the Sun in the eighth house.

Yogini Dasha

He was running Dhanya-Sankata (Jupiter-Rahu).

Birth Chart

Jupiter (Dhanya) the eleventh lord (alternative house of diseases), is placed in the sixth house of accidents.

Rahu (Sankata) is in the seventh house (killer). Rahu's dispositor is the Sun, placed in the eighth house.

From the Moon, Jupiter as the sixth lord of accidents aspects the sixth house also.

Rahu is placed in the eleventh house. Rahu's dispositor the Sun, is placed in the twelfth house of hospitalization with the lagna lord (i.e., the Moon sign lord) Venus.

Navamsha

Jupiter (Dhanya) is the sixth lord placed with the seventh lord Mars (killer). Rahu (Sankata) is also placed with the sixth lord Jupiter. Rahu is more dreadful by placement with violent Mars.

From the Moon, Jupiter (Dhanya) and Rahu (Sankata) are both in the seventh house (killer house).

The prayers of his fans were answered by God and he was saved from the clutches of death.

Case Study 4 :
Accident of Elder Brother (*use of Drekkana*)

Now the same event can be traced in the horoscope of his younger brother. This novel and traditional method has been prevalent in India and the family astrologers who have the horoscopes of the whole family, can always confirm the events from the horoscopes of the relatives.

We will use one divisional chart – Drekkana (Dreshkana) for this purpose.

Vimshottari Dasha

At the time of the accident of his elder brother, the native was running Moon-Mars.

Moon	Mars Venus	Lagna Sun Mercury Rahu	
	Case Four Birth Chart		Saturn
	Ketu	Jupiter (R)	

Lagna	9°48'	Mars	4°31'	Venus	4°23'
Sun	3°07'	Mercury	5°40'	Saturn	10°32'
Moon	28°59'	Jupiter (R)	29°07'	Rahu	9°55'

	Mars Venus	Lagna Sun Mercury Rahu	Jupiter
	Drekkana (D3)		
	Saturn Ketu Moon		

Birth Chart

The Moon is placed in the eleventh house of the elder brother. The sub-period lord Mars is aspecting Jupiter, the eleventh lord.

Take Jupiter as lagna (significator of the elder brother). The Moon is placed in the sixth house of accident. Mars is placed in the seventh house (killer house), with the lagna lord Venus.

Drekkana

Taking Jupiter as the lagna, the major period lord, the Moon, is debilitated and placed in the sixth house of accident. The Moon is conjoined with the eighth lord of fatality Saturn, in Rahu-Ketu axis and aspected by the sixth lord of accidents, Mars.

From Jupiter, the sub-period lord Mars is the sixth lord of accidents placed in the eleventh house of elder brother.

From the Lagna, Mars is also placed with the sixth lord Venus.

Yogini Dasha

Ulka-Bhramari (Saturn-Mars).

Birth Chart

Saturn (Ulka), the major period lord is afflicted by the aspect of violent Mars. Mars (Bhramari) aspects Jupiter, the eleventh lord, representing elder brother.

Taking *Jupiter as the lagna*, Saturn (Ulka) aspects the seventh house and seventh lord Mars. Mars (Bhramari) is the seventh lord placed in the seventh house (double killer), with the eighth lord Venus.

Drekkana

With *Jupiter as the lagna*, Saturn (Ulka) is the eighth lord placed in the sixth house of accidents. Mars (Bhramari) the sixth lord in the eleventh house aspects the sixth house.

Note: Saturn-Mars are placed *shadashtaka* (sixth-eighth) to each other, which is an additional adverse factor.

Case Study 5 :
Selection for a Job (*use of Dashamsha*)

Now it will be shown how the birth chart along with the Dashamsha is used to find the period favourable towards selection for a job.

In such cases the tenth house and the tenth lord are studied invariably from different angles. This is the approach

Lagna		Moon	
Rahu	**Case Five Birth Chart**		
Saturn (R)		Ketu Sun Mercury	
		Venus Mars	Jupiter

		Rahu	
2 Moon	1 Lagna	11	10 Saturn (R)
	12 3 9 6		
4 5 Ketu Sun Mercury	Jupiter		7 8 Venus Mars

Lagna	5°20'	Mars	17°47'	Venus	2°16'
Sun	25°26'	Mercury	25°06'	Saturn (R)	17°40'
Moon	22°00'	Jupiter	7°21'	Rahu	5°46'

Mars Rahu	Sun Mercury		
Saturn	**Dashamsha (D10)**		Jupiter
			Moon
Lagna		Venus	Ketu

11 Saturn	10 Lagna	8	7 Venus
Mars Rahu	12 9 3 6		Ketu
1 Sun Mercury	2	4 Jupiter	5 Moon

consistently followed in the previous chapters also. The following points are considered in the analysis.

(a) the tenth house from the lagna.

(b) the tenth lord from the lagna.

(c) the tenth house from the Moon.

(d) the tenth lord from the Moon.

(e) An additional but useful house, often ignored, is the seventh house. Planets linked with the seventh house give position of status. Maharshi Parashara describes seventh house as the house of *pada-prapti* (getting a high post).

Note: The seventh house is tenth from the tenth house, so it becomes an alternative house of profession.

(f) The dasha running at the time of career-making age is also important, as it gives new twists and turns to the career.

Analyse the above points both in the birth chart and in the Dashamsha.

Vimshottari Dasha

This native got the dasha balance of Moon (11 months and 25 days) at birth. This was followed by 7 years of Mars dasha. Thus from 8 years to 26 years of age, he had 18 years of Rahu dasha. Now, analyse Rahu:

Rahu is placed in the twelfth house, aspected by the sixth lord of struggles and competition, the Sun. The dispositor of Rahu is Saturn. Saturn is placed in the eleventh house of gains, aspected by the tenth lord Jupiter, and the ninth lord of luck, Mars. After completing his education, the native was ready to pursue a career. Hence, the dasha in progress matters. He was in the fag end of Rahu's major period and the sub-period of Mars.

From the Moon, Rahu is in the tenth house aspected by the Sun, the significator of the government. The sub-period lord Mars aspects the tenth lord Saturn from the sixth house of competition.

Dashamsha
Rahu and Mars both are placed in the fourth house, aspecting the tenth house.

Yogini Dasha

Now use Yogini dasha as an additional tool to cross check.

Yogini dasha was of Ulka-Siddha (Saturn-Venus).

Birth Chart

Saturn (Ulka) is aspected by the tenth lord Jupiter.

Venus (Siddha) is aspected by the eleventh lord of achievement, Saturn. Venus is also placed with the ninth lord of luck, Mars in the eighth house.

Note: Saturn (Ulka) and Venus (Siddha) are placed in fourth-tenth position from each other (good for career).

From the Moon, Saturn is the tenth lord placed in the ninth house. Venus in the sixth house is aspected by the tenth lord Saturn.

Dashamsha

Saturn (Ulka) and Venus (Siddha) both also aspect the tenth lord Mercury. Venus is also the sixth lord.

Note: (i) Saturn and Venus are placed fifth-ninth to each other (again favourable).

(ii) Saturn and Venus both aspect the seventh lord Mercury (giver of a position).

The time was ripe, the dasha was appropriate. The native was selected for a job in the Indian Police Service through an All India Competitive Examination.

Case Study 6 :
Rise in Career (*use of Dashamsha*)

In August 1990, he was expecting to be elevated to a very high post. The prediction given to him was that he would get a high post, but not in the main line of his profession.

Vimshottari Dasha

He was running the major period of Saturn and the sub-period of Jupiter.

Case Six Birth Chart (South Indian style)

			Lagna
Rahu	**Case Six Birth Chart**		Ketu
Saturn			Ketu
	Mars Venus	Sun Mercury	Jupiter Moon

(North Indian style chart)

5 Ketu · 4 · Lagna · 2 · 1 · Jupiter Moon 3 · 6 12 · 9 · 7 Sun Mercury · 8 Mars Venus · 10 Saturn · 11 Rahu

Lagna	10°28'	Mars 13°39' Venus 15°42'
Sun	1°54'	Mercury 23°59' Saturn 16°48'
Moon	24°33'	Jupiter 15°20' Rahu 4°09'

Dashamsha (D10) (South Indian style)

Rahu		Mercury	
Saturn	**Dashamsha (D10)**		
Moon			
Venus	Mars	Sun Jupiter	Lagna Ketu

(North Indian style chart)

8 Sun Jupiter · 7 · Mars · Lagna Ketu · 5 · 4 · Venus 6 · 9 3 · 12 · 10 Moon · Rahu · 11 · 1 · 2 Mercury · Saturn

Saturn the eighth lord in the eighth house aspects the tenth house, showing a break in his present activities. The sub-period lord Jupiter, as the tenth lord, aspects the tenth house. Jupiter is also involved in an excellent Gaja Kesari Yoga. (This yoga is formed when the Moon and Jupiter are in kendra from each other, a yoga which confers authority.)

Dashamsha

The major period lord Saturn is in its own house, but in the sixth house.

The sub-period lord Jupiter aspects the tenth house.

Note: An indication for change is also there if we concentrate on the tenth house. The tenth house and the tenth lord Mercury both are aspected by the eighth lord Mars.

Instead of becoming number one man in the service, he was given another post, of the rank of a State Minister.

His grand luck continued and in the middle of 1991 he became the Chief Adviser to a very important man in power in India.

Yogini Dasha

He was running Siddha-Siddha (Venus-Venus).

Venus (Siddha) is the fifth lord of dignity in the birth horoscope. The fifth lord, according to Parashara, is a minister.

Dashamsha

Venus (Siddha) is the ninth lord in the fourth house (Sagittarius), aspecting the tenth house of profession.

Note: In the Siddha period, his daughter was also selected for Indian Administrative Services. Venus is the fifth lord of children in the birth horoscope.

Case Study 7 :
Birth of the Children (*use of Saptamsha*)

Saptamsha is the divisional chart relevant to progeny. Birth of children and other matters related to their health, career and the like are to be judged from the Saptamsha too, in addition to the fifth house and fifth lord of the rashi chart. Here we shall consider the application of the Yogini dasha, along with the Vimshottari, using the Saptamsha as an additional divisional chart, to decipher birth of children.

We are taking an example horoscope of a female.

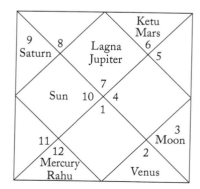

Case Seven Birth Chart (South Indian)

Saturn Mars Rahu			Moon
Mercury (R)			
Sun			Jupiter (R)
Venus		Lagna	Ketu

Case Seven Birth Chart (North Indian)
- 9 Venus · 8 · Lagna · Ketu · 6 · 5 Jupiter (R)
- 7 · Sun · 10 · 4 · 1
- 11 Mercury (R) · 12 Saturn Mars Rahu · 2 · 3 Moon

Lagna	0°35'	Mars	0°54'
Sun	26°38'	Mercury (R)	8°03'
Moon	1°52'	Jupiter (R)	8°52'

Venus	23°43'
Saturn	15°31'
Rahu	27°25'

Navamsha (D9) (South Indian)

Rahu			Jupiter
			Mars
			Sun
Mercury	Saturn Venus	Lagna Moon	Ketu

Navamsha (D9) (North Indian)
- 9 Mercury · 8 Saturn Venus · Lagna Moon · Ketu · 6 · 5 Sun
- 7 · 10 · 4 Mars · 1
- 11 · 12 · Rahu · 2 · 3 Jupiter

Saptamsha (D7) (South Indian)

Mercury Rahu	Venus		Moon
Sun			
Saturn		Lagna Jupiter	Ketu Mars

Saptamsha (D7) (North Indian)
- 9 Saturn · 8 · Lagna Jupiter · Ketu Mars · 6 · 5
- 7 · Sun · 10 · 4 · 1
- 11 · 12 Mercury Rahu · 2 Venus · 3 Moon

115

To study the promise of birth of children, check the following points in the horoscope:

(a) The fifth house and the aspects on fifth house

(b) The fifth lord, the aspects on the fifth lord, the conjunctions with the fifth lord.

(c) The strength of Jupiter, the significator for children.

Study the points (a), (b) and (c) from (i) Lagna (ii) Jupiter (iii) Navamsha lagna (iv) Saptamsha lagna.

From	Fifth house	Fifth lord	Jupiter
Lagna	Aquarius. Has 9th lord Mer. aspected by 6th lord Jupiter – promises progeny with difficulties.	5th lord Saturn in 6th house: bad; with it's enemy: bad; with Mars: bad; in Rahu-Ketu axis: bad.	In Leo in *alpasuta* rashi* (a rashi not promising many children) aspected by 9th lord Mer.
Jupiter as Lagna	Sagittarius has 3rd and 10th lord Venus aspected by the 12th lord Moon; also aspected by the 6th lord Sat from 8th creating difficulty.	5th lord Jupiter is retrograde, and is aspected by retrograde Mercury – a cause for caution.	
Navamsha Lagna	Aquarius – aspected by two malefics Mars and Sun – obstacles; also aspected by Jupiter – protects the house.	5th lord Saturn in Scorpio (an inimical sign) with Venus, its friend; but Venus is the 8th lord of hindrance.	In the rashi of Mercury (Gemini) in the 9th house, aspected by the 9th lord Mercury.
Saptamsha Lagna	Aquarius aspected by Jupiter – good, and Saturn – its own lord, is alright.	5th lord Saturn in Sagittarius, a neutral sign, aspected by Moon – alright; aspected by its enemy Mars – not good.	In lagna in Libra sign unaspected by any planet but aspects the 5th house.

Note: Role of Mercury – Eunuch – reduces chances of fertility, as it is a sterile planet.

* Taurus, Leo, Virgo and Scorpio are considered *alpa-suta* rashis, not promising many children.

Conclusions

(a) There are a few negative features regarding the child birth.

(b) Relief is available by Jupiter's benevolent aspect

(c) What Jupiter determines, is the birth of child.

Vimshottari Dasha Sequence

This female got married in the Vimshottari dasha of Jupiter-Saturn. We will analyse this dasha for the promise of children.

Jupiter-Saturn

Birth Chart

Jupiter is aspecting the fifth house. Sub-period lord Saturn is the fifth lord, placed in the sixth house of hurdles, is also with its enemy Mars. This affliction is increased by Rahu-Ketu axis.

Navamsha

Jupiter is aspecting the fifth house. Saturn is the fifth lord, placed with the eighth lord Venus — may create difficulty.

Saptamsha

Jupiter in the Saptamsha Lagna aspects the fifth house also. Saturn is the fifth lord, aspected by its enemy Mars, an instigator of miscarriages.

We notice that the major period of Jupiter is helpful, as visible in all the charts, but the sub-period of Saturn is not fruitful, as Saturn is afflicted in all the above charts.

The conclusions drawn above are right, as she had two abortions in Jupiter-Saturn period.

The Next period was of Jupiter-Mercury.

118

Jupiter-Mercury

Birth Chart
Jupiter in eleventh and Mercury in the fifth house – both are child giving houses.

Navamsha
Jupiter aspects the fifth house, Mercury is the ninth lord (an alternative house of children, fifth from the fifth house)

Saptamsha
Jupiter in the lagna aspects the fifth house. Mercury is the ninth lord, but debilitated.

This period proved fruitful, and she gave birth to a female child after prolonged labour pains. The delivery was normal.

Note: The lagna of a divisional chart is also important in fructifying the promise of the relevant divisional chart. Thus Jupiter in the lagna of the Saptamsha would be helpful in the birth of children during its dasha (just as a planet in the lagna of the Navamsha chart would promise marriage or relationship during its dasha). Same rule applies to other divisional charts also.

Yogini Dasha

Period of Abortions
Both the abortions took place in Ulka (Saturn) major period. Saturn as the fifth lord in the sixth house, as an obstacle, has already been discussed.

Child Birth Period
Siddha-Sankata (Venus-Rahu)

Birth Chart
From the lagna, Venus (Siddha) is aspected by the fifth lord Saturn and by Jupiter, the natural significator of

children. Rahu (Sankata) is with the 5th lord Saturn. Rahu's dispositor is Jupiter, aspecting the 5th house.

From Jupiter, Venus (Siddha) is in fifth house. Rahu (Sankata) is with the ninth lord Mars. Rahu's dispositor is Jupiter.

Note: Analyse the dasha taking the child giver, Jupiter, as the lagna. The first, the fifth and the ninth houses *from Jupiter* are child giving houses.

Navamsha

From the lagna, Venus (Siddha) is with the fifth lord Saturn. Rahu (Sankata) is in the sixth house, but its dispositor is Jupiter, which aspects the fifth house.

From Jupiter, Venus is the fifth lord. Rahu in the sign of Jupiter is acting as Jupiter.

Saptamsha

Venus is the lagna lord. Rahu is with the ninth lord in the sign of Jupiter.

Case Study 8 :
Children going abroad for a job (*use of Saptamsha*)

It is always easy to give predictions with accurate timing if horoscopes made on accurate birth time are available. It becomes easier if the horoscopes of other family members are known.

That is what family astrologers have been doing exceedingly well in India since older times. It is just like what a 'Family Doctor' does when he treats a patient, taking into account his family's medical history also. An astrologer, if technically sound, can always confirm the events from the horoscopes of family members. Various divisional charts can be used effectively while doing this.

In this case, we will study the career prospects of the children of a person seeking astrologer's guidance. How

Case Eight Birth Chart (South Indian style)

Moon			Ketu
Saturn	**Case Eight Birth Chart**		
Lagna			
Rahu Jupiter Venus	Sun Mercury		Mars

(North Indian style chart)

Houses: 12 Moon / 11 / Lagna / 10 / 1 / 7 / 4 / Rahu (in 12 area with Moon) / Saturn; Rahu Jupiter Venus 9 / Sun Mercury 8; Mars 6; Ketu 2/3; 5

Lagna	14°23'	
Sun	8°48'	
Moon	7°05'	

Mars	12°45'		Venus	13°15'	
Mercury	12°04'		Saturn	22°51'	
Jupiter	5°15'		Rahu	2°29'	

Saptamsha (D7) (South Indian style)

Venus		Mars	Ketu
	Saptamsha (D7)		Mercury Saturn Sun
Jupiter			
Rahu		Lagna Moon	

(North Indian style D7 chart)

Houses: 9 Rahu / 8 / Lagna Moon / 6 / 5; Jupiter 10 / 7 / 4 Mercury Saturn Sun / 1; 11 / 12 / 2 Ketu / 3; Venus; Mars

accurate divisional charts, combined with at least two dasha systems, become dependable tools of Vedic astrology, will be shown now.

See the combinations in the horoscope given below which clearly hint about the native's children going abroad for a job.

Birth Chart

(a) The fifth lord of children is in the twelfth house of foreign countries with the twelfth lord.

(b) *From Jupiter*, the significator for children, twelfth lord is in the tenth house of profession, and tenth lord is in the twelfth house.

Saptamsha

(a) The fifth lord Saturn is in tenth house with Mercury, the twelfth lord.

(b) Exalted lagna lord in the sixth house is aspecting the twelfth house.

Vimshottari Dasha

In September 1983, the native was running Venus-Rahu. Venus is the fifth lord placed in the twelfth house with the twelfth lord Jupiter.

Rahu is also in the twelfth house with the fifth lord of the children.

Now see another approach. Take Jupiter (*putrakaraka*) as the lagna.

The Major period lord Venus and sub-period lord Rahu are in the lagna, aspected by Mars, the lord of the fifth house as well as the twelfth house.

See the Saptamsha now for confirmation:

The major period lord Venus is the lagna lord, exalted in the sixth house of contracts, aspecting the twelfth house.

The sub-period lord Rahu is aspecting the ninth house of luck.

Note: Rahu's connection with the ninth house often gives links with foreigners.

An observation: Sub-period of Rahu often separates the native from his family.

In the above period, native's first child, a chemical engineer, went abroad having picked up a job.

In February 1993, the native was running Venus-Mercury.

The major period of Venus was always favourable for his children.

The sub-period lord Mercury is the ninth lord (an alternative house of children), placed in the eleventh house of gains.

122

Note: No apparent foreign connection is visible here. However, with Jupiter as the lagna, Mercury is the tenth lord placed in the twelfth house.

In the Saptamsha, the sub-period lord Mercury is again the twelfth lord of foreign country, placed in the tenth house of profession.

In Venus-Mercury his second child, a medical doctor, went abroad.

Yogini Dasha

Now we take Yogini Dasha to clinch the prediction.

Siddha-Siddha (Venus-Venus)
Venus as the fifth lord in the twelfth house has already been discussed. It coincides with the major period of Vimshottari dasha. His first child went abroad in this period only.

Sankata-Bhramari (Rahu-Mars)
The placement of Rahu with the fifth lord of the birth chart and the connection of Rahu with the ninth house of Saptamsha chart have been discussed.

Birth Chart
The sub-period lord Mars (Bhramari) aspects the fifth lord Venus who is placed in the twelfth house.

Saptamsha
Mars (Bhramari) is the seventh lord (tenth from the tenth house).

Note: *From Jupiter as the lagna* in the Saptamsha, Mars (Bhramari) is placed in the fifth house, and is also aspecting the twelfth house. Mars is also being aspected by the twelfth lord Jupiter.

In Sankata-Bhramari, his second child got the opportunity to go to a foreign country for a job.

Case Study 9 :
Period of Distinction for father (*use of Dwadashamsha*)

This is the horoscope of a person whose father became the Prime Minister of his country within five years of his birth.

This horoscope should have:

(a) the combinations for rise of father, and

(b) a good dasha for father.

Moon	Sun	Lagna Saturn Venus Mercury	Jupiter
Mars		**Case Nine Birth Chart**	Rahu
Ketu			

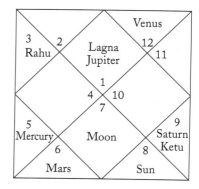

Lagna	28°38'	Mars	17°59'	Venus	26°03'
Sun	17°44'	Mercury	8°15'	Saturn	18°20'
Moon	19°00'	Jupiter	25°57'	Rahu	28°23'

Venus	Lagna Jupiter		Rahu
	Dwadashamsha (D12)		Mercury
Saturn Ketu	Sun	Moon	Mars

124

Some Indications for the high position of the father

(a) The significator for father, the Sun, is exalted.

(b) Saturn the ninth lord, signifying father, is placed in the lagna with Mercury the fifth lord of dignity, and the lagna lord Venus.

(c) The ninth house *from the Sun* is aspected by the ninth lord Jupiter providing strength to it.

(d) Taking the *ninth house Capricorn as the lagna* of father, the tenth lord (representing position held by father) Venus is with Mercury the ninth lord of luck.

Indications in Dwadashamsha

(a) The tenth lord of distinction is placed in the ninth house of father.

(b) The ninth house is aspected by the ninth lord Jupiter, making the father's house stronger.

(c) Take *the Sun as the lagna* for the father. The tenth house is aspected by the fifth lord Jupiter.

Vimshottari Dasha

The Native was running Mercury-Moon.

Birth Chart

Mercury is placed in the lagna (has directional strength), with the ninth lord of father, Saturn.

The Moon is placed in the eleventh house of gains.

Note: The Moon aspects the fifth house (the ninth from the ninth house) which is the house of luck for the father.

From the Sun, Mercury is placed with Saturn the tenth lord of distinction. Moon is the fourth lord which represents Parliament.

Does Dwadashamsha Chart Help?

The major-period lord Mercury aspects the eleventh house of achievement. The sub-period lord Moon is the fourth lord of simhasana (seat of power) in the seventh house of position.

From the Sun, Moon is the ninth lord of luck, aspected by Jupiter the fifth lord of dignity.

Yogini Dasha

The native was running Ulka-Siddha (Saturn-Venus).

Birth Chart

Saturn (Ulka) is the ninth lord of father, placed in the lagna with the lagna lord, Venus (Siddha).

From the Sun, Saturn (Ulka) is the tenth lord of distinction, and Venus (Siddha) is with the tenth lord.

Dwadashamsha

Saturn (Ulka) is placed in the ninth house of father, aspected by the ninth lord Jupiter. Venus (Siddha) the seventh lord of position is exalted.

From the Sun, Saturn (Ulka) is in the royal sign*, aspected by the fifth lord Jupiter. Venus (Siddha) is the seventh lord of position, exalted in the fifth house of dignity.

Case Study 10 :
Father's Death (*use of Dwadashamsha*)

Numerous combinations are given by Parashara for the fatality of father. Some of them are:

(a) The Sun in the sixth, eighth or twelfth house and eighth lord in the ninth house.

(b) The Sun in the eighth house with the ninth lord.

---

* Leo and Sagittarius are considered royal signs. Observe placement of planets in these two rashis.

(c) Twelfth lord in the ninth house and the ninth lord debilitated.

Some special combinations

(d) Rahu in the fourth house (eighth *from the ninth house*) and Sun in the fifth house (ninth *from the ninth house*).

(e) Exchange of twelfth lord and the ninth lord.

(f) The third house has the Sun and the ninth house has Rahu.

(g) The second house has Sun and the eighth house has Saturn.

The essence of all such combinations for the fatality to the father is:

(a) affliction to the significator of father, the Sun.

(b) affliction to the ninth house of father by the sixth, eighth or twelfth lords.
    Note: Pay special attention to the affliction of the ninth house by the eighth lord.

(c) affliction along the ninth and the third house axis (it becomes one-seven axis for father).

(d) affliction along the second house and eighth house axis (it becomes sixth house and twelfth house axis for father).

(e) affliction to the fifth house (ninth *from the ninth house*, an alternative house of father).

These combinations with modifications may be present in the Birth Chart, Navamsha and Dwadashamsha.

Involvement of malefics further reduces the life span of father.

Operation of a dasha fatal for father will always remain important, to time the period of danger to the father.

Death of the father can occur in the dashas of the:

(a) Planets posited in the second house and seventh house, counted *from the ninth house.*

(b) Planets posited in the second house and the seventh house counted *from the Sun.*

(c) Planetary lords of the above houses.

(d) Planets conjunct with or aspected by the killer planets for father.

(e) Planets causing affliction to the ninth house.

Let us take an example horoscope:

			Saturn Sun Venus Ketu
Mars		Lagna	
Moon	**Case Ten** **Birth Chart**		Mercury
Jupiter (R)			
Rahu			

Lagna	11°50'	Mars	7°51'	Venus	27°26'
Sun	7°50'	Mercury	2°57'	Saturn	1°36'
Moon	26°56'	Jupiter (R)	17°49'	Rahu	14°37'

North Indian chart: Saturn Sun Venus Ketu (4,3 Mercury), Lagna, 1/12 Mars, 2, 5/11 Moon, 8, 10 Jupiter (R), 6, 7, 9 Rahu.

	Venus	Rahu	Mars Saturn
	Dwadashamsha (D12)		
			Jupiter Mercury
Moon	Ketu		Lagna Sun

North Indian chart D12: 8 Ketu, 7, Lagna Sun, Jupiter Mercury 5, 4, Moon 9, 6, 3 Mars Saturn, 12, 10, 11, 1, 2 Rahu, Venus.

See the following combination for father's fatality present in the Birth Chart.

(a) the eighth lord Jupiter is in the ninth house retrograde and debilitated.

(b) the second house (sixth house *from the ninth house* of father) is heavily afflicted.

(c) The Sun is afflicted.

(d) The ninth lord Saturn is afflicted.

(e) Instead of Sun-Saturn in the second-eighth house axis, we have Sun with Saturn in the second house and Rahu aspecting both from the eighth house.

Now study Dwadashamsha separately.

(a) The Sun is afflicted by the eighth lord Mars.

(b) The ninth lord from the lagna and the Sun is Venus, placed in the eighth house.

Vimshottari Dasha

The native was running Saturn-Moon when he was 19 years old. During this period his father expired.

Birth Chart

Saturn the ninth lord is with the sixth lord of accidents, Venus. The violent Mars aspects the fourth lord (Sun) of vehicles who is with Saturn. The native's father died in a vehicular accident.

The sub-period lord Moon is the lord of the third house of longevity of the parents.

Why is the Moon killer for father?

(a) The Moon is the seventh lord from the ninth house.

(b) The Moon is the second lord from the Sun.

(c) The Moon is placed in the second house from the ninth house.

Dwadashamsha

Treat the Sun as the lagna. Mahadasha lord Saturn being the sixth lord of accidents aspects the fourth house and the fourth lord Jupiter. It is a typical combination for vehicular accident. Saturn is also placed with the eighth lord Mars, making it more dreaded.

The sub-period lord Moon is in the fourth house aspected by the sixth and eighth lords, Saturn and Mars.

Yogini Dasha

He was running Siddha-Ulka (Venus-Saturn).

Birth Chart

Venus (Siddha) is the sixth lord of accidents placed with the ninth lord Saturn, and the significator of the father, the Sun.

Saturn (Ulka) is the ninth lord placed with the sixth lord Venus.

Note: Venus and Saturn are together in the second house (sixth house from the ninth house).

Dwadashamsha

Venus (Siddha) is the ninth lord placed in the eighth house. Saturn (Ulka) is the sixth lord, placed with the eighth lord Mars, and aspects the lagna lord Mercury.

CHAPTER ELEVEN

COMPOSITE APPROACH OF VEDIC ASTROLOGY

A criticism of the Yogini dasha is that its cycle, being only for 36 years, proves inapplicable after 36 years of age. According to the astrologers of Jammu, the northern state of India, the cycle of Yogini dasha should be repeated after the completion of previous cycle. So the first cycle of Yogini dasha will run up to 36 years of age, the second cycle up to 72 years and the third cycle up to 108 years of age. So the benefic and malefic periods of one cycle will repeat in the second and the third cycles also but the results will get modified according to the transit of planets during that period.

Interpreting Transits (Our Approach)

Whenever any important event is happening in the life of a person, Jupiter and Saturn in transit play a very important role. When both Jupiter and Saturn in transit influence a house, activities related to that house start happening.

Saturn is the *kaala* (the cosmic clock), without whose permission no event, good or bad, can take place. Saturn permits the house to fructify its significations by being placed there, or by its aspect on that house. Jupiter is the divine lord who blesses and confers grace to the event. Mars is the planet authorised to execute the orders of Saturn and Jupiter. The month of the event is controlled by the Sun and the day by the Moon.

In analysing the transit of planets with reference to the significations of any house, treat *the house as the lagna* and see the position of transiting planets. Planets transiting in the benefic houses are favourable and in the malefic houses unfavourable.

Transit from the Moon Lagna

The traditional method of analysing the results of the transiting planets is from the Moon lagna. The rashi where the Moon is positioned in the birth chart is treated as the Moon lagna and the results of the transiting planets depend on their position *with reference to the Moon lagna*. Transiting planets in different positions from the natal Moon are favourable or unfavourable.

Transiting Planet			*Position from the natal Moon*								
The Sun	: *Favourable* :	3/9	6/12	10/4	11/5						
	*Vedha** :										
The Moon	: *Favourable* :	1/5	3/9	6/12	7/2	10/4	11/8				
	Vedha :										
Mars	: *Favourable* :	3/12	6/9	11/5							
	Vedha :										
Mercury	: *Favourable* :	2/5	4/3	6/9	8/1	10/7	11/12				
	Vedha :										
Jupiter	: *Favourable* :	2/12	5/4	7/3	9/10	11/8					
	Vedha :										
Venus	: *Favourable* :	1/8	2/7	3/1	4/10	5/9	8/5	9/11	11/6	12/3	
	Vedha :										
Saturn	: *Favourable* :	3/12	6/9	11/5							
	Vedha :										

* Obstruction

If a transiting planet is in a favourable position from the natal Moon and simultaneously another planet is traveling in the Vedha position, the result will no longer be favour-able. For example transiting Sun is favourable in the third house from the natal Moon. However, if simultaneously Mars is transiting in ninth (vedha) house, the Sun will no longer be favourable.

Exception : No vedha occurs between the Sun and Saturn, and the Moon and Mercury.

Special Principles of Transiting Planets

Here is a collection of some principles as given in classical texts. A thorough research is needed before adopting these principles in general use.

(1) Planets during their transit in a sign give results at different periods: the Sun and Mars in the beginning of a sign; Venus and Jupiter in the middle of a sign; the Moon and Saturn at the end of a sign and Mercury always gives results irrespective of its position.

(2) Planets start giving the results of the next sign even before entering the sign as shown below:

The Moon – 3 ghatis (1 hour 12 minutes); the Sun – 5 days; Mercury – 7 days; Venus – 7 days; Mars – 8 days; Jupiter – 2 months; Rahu – 3 months; Saturn – 6 months before entering the sign, start giving the results of the sign being entered.

(3) Planets inflict pain to the following parts of the body when they are unfavourable in transit: the Sun – head; the Moon – throat, chest; Mars – back, stomach; Mercury – arms, legs; Jupiter – waist, thighs; Venus – anus, testicles; Saturn – knees, joints.

(4) The interpretation of dasha should be done from the birth chart and also from the transit position of planets at the time of beginning of the particular dasha. At the time of beginning of a dasha if the transiting planets

are in benefic houses (kendra, trikona, etc.) the dasha will prove favourable; if in malefic houses (sixth, eighth, twelfth, etc.) the dasha will be unfavourable.

(5) Here is a collection of some principles as given in the *Phaladeepika* by Mantreshwara. The results pertaining to the house under consideration are achieved on the fulfillment of the following conditions:

(a) The principle is based on the movement of the lagna lord and house lord (whose results are under observation).

   (i) When the lagna lord passes through the house under consideration.

   (ii) When the lagna lord and the house lord get conjoined or aspect each other in transit.

   (iii) When the lagna lord passes in trine to the house occupied by the house lord.

   (iv) When the lagna lord is in trine to the Navamsha sign occupied by the house lord.

   (v) When the house lord passes through the sign which is in trine to the Navamsha sign occupied by the lagna lord.

   (vi) When the significator of the house under consideration gets conjoined with the lagna lord.

   (vii) When the significator of the house under consideration gets conjoined with the Moon sign lord.

(b) When Jupiter in transit is in trine to the sign occupied by the house lord under consideration in:

   (i) Birth chart

   (ii) Navamsha

Three Cycles of Yogini Dasha

In this chapter we are taking three case studies and analysing the events, retrospectively, by applying two dashas – Vimshottari and Yogini, relevant divisional charts and the transit position of planets at the time of occurrence of the event concerned.

The first example is that of Sanjay Gandhi (second son of Mrs. Indira Gandhi, late prime minister of India) which covers the first cycle (36 years) of Yogini dasha. The second example is of John F. Kennedy (late president of USA) covering the two cycles of Yogini Dasha. The third example is of Jawaharlal Nehru (first prime minister of India) covering the three cycles of Yogini dasha. We are also providing here the birth data of the natives for the convenience of the readers.

Case One: Sanjay Gandhi

Born on December 14, 1946, at 9:27 hours (IST) at Delhi, India.

Sanjay Gandhi was an Indian politician and a family member of the Nehru-Gandhi dynasty. During his lifetime he was widely expected to succeed his mother, Indira Gandhi, as head of the Indian National Congress, but following his early death in a plane crash his elder brother Rajiv became their mother's political heir, and succeeded her as Prime Minister of India after her death.

Salient Features of the Horoscope

1. Ascendant being Capricorn, is aspected by its own lord, Saturn, though retrograde. Ascendant lord, Saturn, is in the seventh house aspected by its enemy Mars. The Moon is in the adverse eighth house.

    The Sun is in Rahu-Ketu axis, with Mercury, a malefic in this case.

Sanjay Gandhi (First Cycle of Yogini Dasha)

Born on December 14, 1946, at 9:27 hours (IST) at Delhi, India.

Sanjay Gandhi Birth Chart (South Indian style)

		Rahu	
	Sanjay Gandhi Birth Chart		Saturn (R)
Lagna			Moon
Mars	Mercury Sun Ketu	Jupiter Venus	

Birth Chart (North Indian style): 12 / 11 / Lagna; Mars, Sun, Mercury, Ketu (9, 8); Jupiter Venus (10, 1, 7, 4); Rahu (2, 3); Saturn (R); Moon (5, 6).

Lagna	1°24'	Mars	4°21'	Venus	24°16'
Sun	28°18'	Mercury	8°11'	Saturn	15°26'
Moon	12°30'	Jupiter	23°51'	Rahu	18°35'

Navamsha (D9) (South Indian style)

Sun		Jupiter Venus Mars	Rahu
	Navamsha (D9)		Moon
Lagna			
Ketu	Saturn		Mercury

Navamsha (D9) (North Indian style): 12 Sun / 11 / Lagna; Ketu (9, 8); Saturn (10, 1, 7, 4); Jupiter Venus Mars (2, 3); Moon; Mercury (5, 6); Rahu.

Dashamsha (D10) (South Indian style)

	Sun	Jupiter	Venus
	Dashamsha (D10)		Rahu
Mars Ketu			Saturn
Moon			Lagna Mercury

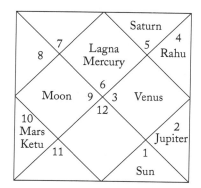

Dashamsha (D10) (North Indian style): 8 / 7 / Lagna Mercury; Saturn (5, 4); Rahu; Moon (9, 6, 3, 12); Venus; Mars Ketu (10, 11); Jupiter (2, 1); Sun.

			Ketu
Mercury	**Dwadashamsha**		Jupiter Venus
Lagna Mars Saturn Moon	**(D12)**		
Rahu		Sun	

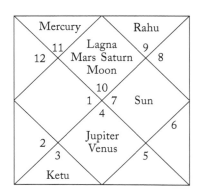

The essence of 'Lagna-Moon-Sun' analysis is the influence of Saturn-Mars, as well as eighth house-twelfth house, predominantly on the native. This fact is also highlighted in the Navamsha where the lagna lord is again Saturn, in the sign of Mars, aspected by its lord Mars. Jupiter-Venus also influence the lagna lord in the Navamsha.

2. Two benefics Jupiter and Venus and a malefic Saturn, in the quadrants giving more than the moderate strength to the lagna.

   Lack of benefic planets in the Trines, denies the native the protective shield of 'Purva Punya' in the times of disaster.

3. Planets get concentrated in the visible half of the horoscope that is from the seventh house to the twelfth house, indicating a fairly active social life of the native.

4. *Rajayogas*

   (a) The fifth lord in the tenth house is a combination of authority, though blemished by the association of the twelfth lord Jupiter. The native enjoyed a very small span of power, when he remained 'Member of Parliament' for six months period.

   (b) The fifth lord of dignity aspects the fourth house of mother. Two most benefic planets aspect the fourth house. The mother of the native was a dignitary, the Prime Minister of India.

5. *Arishta Yogas*

   (i) The sixth and the eighth lords in the eleventh house.

   (ii) The third and the twelfth lord in the tenth house.

Table of Events

	Date	Event	Vimshottari	Yogini
1.	Sep. 8, 1960	Father died	Venus-Saturn	Sankata-Sankata (Rahu-Rahu)
2.	Jan. 24, 1966	Mother became Prime Minister	Venus-Mercury	Sankata-Ulka (Rahu-Saturn)
3.	Sep. 23, 1974	Marriage	Moon-Mars	Bhramari-Bhadrika (Mars-Mercury)
4.	Mar. 21, 1977	Mother lost in election	Moon-Jupiter	Bhramari-Sankata (Mars-Rahu)
5.	January 1980	Elected to Parliament	Moon-Mercury	Bhadrika-Siddha (Mercury-Venus)
6.	June 23, 1980	Died in air crash	Mon-Mer-Sat	Bhadrika-Siddha (Mercury-Venus)

Event No. 1 :
Father Feroz Gandhi Died (September 8, 1960)

The young boy at the age of fourteen lost his father. His father Feroze Gandhi died after suffering a second heart attack. The combinations which are bad (arishtas) for the longevity of father have been discussed in chapter X (case study 10). Let's analyse the arishtas for father in this horoscope.

(i) The ninth lord Mercury is associated with the eighth lord, the Sun. (This arishta was especially emphasised earlier).

(ii) The Sun, the significator for father, is in Rahu-Ketu axis.

(iii)*From the Sun*, the ninth house has retrograde Saturn aspected by the sixth lord Mars.

(iv) *In Navamsha* the ninth lord Mercury, though exalted, is aspected by the eighth lord, the Sun.

(v) *In Dwadashamsha*, the significator of father, the Sun, the eighth lord, is debilitated, and is aspected by its enemy, Saturn.

Vimshottari Dasha : Venus-Saturn

Birth Chart
Venus, the major period lord is not connected with the ninth house directly but Saturn, the sub-period lord, aspects the ninth house of father.

From the Sun, Venus is the seventh lord (killer), placed with the second lord (killer) Jupiter in the twelfth house. Retrograde Saturn is placed in the ninth house of father, aspected by the sixth lord Mars from the second house (maraka house).

Dwadashamsha
From the Sun, Venus is the lagna lord, placed with the sixth lord Jupiter and also aspected by the two malefics, Mars and Saturn.

Why did the sub-period lord Saturn prove to be a killer? Because Saturn is with Mars which is a double killer in this case being the second and the seventh lord.

Note: According to Parashara, if Saturn is associated with the killer planets, it overrides them and becomes a killer itself.

Yogini Dasha : Sankata-Sankata (Rahu-Rahu)

Birth Chart
Rahu afflicts the ninth lord Mercury and the Sun. *From the Sun*, Rahu is in the seventh house (killer), aspected by the eighth lord Mercury.

Dwadashamsha

From the Sun, Rahu is in the third house, thus aspects the ninth house of father. Rahu's dispositor Jupiter is the sixth lord, placed with the lagna lord, Venus. Affliction of Jupiter is intensified by the aspect of Mars, acting as a killer for father.

Transit

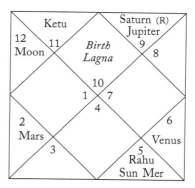

Moon		Mars	
Ketu	**Transit Chart** Sep. 8, 1960		Rahu Sun Mercury
Birth Lagna			
Saturn (R) Jupiter			Venus

The day the father of the boy died, Saturn after passing over his natal Sun (from its previous house, being retrograde) was aspecting his ninth house. Transiting Mars was aspecting his ninth lord Mercury in the eleventh house. Rahu and Sun were in Leo, afflicting the ninth lord, the Moon, *from the natal Sun.*

Note: Please note that planets during their transit, when retrograde, exert influence from the previous house also.

Event No. 2 :
**Mother Indira Gandhi became the
Prime Minister of India** (January 24, 1966)

Following the death of Indian Prime Minister Lal Bahadur Shastri, Indira Gandhi became head of the Congress Party and thus prime minister of India. Let's analyse Sanjay's dashas to see prospects for his mother.

Vimshottari Dasha : Venus-Mercury

Birth Chart

Venus the fifth lord (as well as the tenth lord) placed in tenth house (kendra) is a yogakaraka. Venus aspects the fourth house of mother and Mercury, the sub-period lord, is the ninth lord of luck, so a favourable period.

From the Moon, the significator of mother, Venus is the tenth lord of distinction. Mercury is the eleventh lord (achievements) posited in the fourth house of parliament, aspecting the tenth house of profession.

Dwadashamsha

From the Moon, Venus is the tenth lord of profession, placed in the seventh house of position. Mercury as the ninth lord, had to bestow good fortune.

Yogini Dasha : Sankata-Ulka (Rahu-Saturn)

Birth Chart

Rahu, placed in one trikona, aspected by another trikona lord had to prove favourable.

Rahu's dispositor is Venus. Both Venus and Saturn aspect the fourth house, indicating mother.

From the Moon, Rahu (Sankata) is placed in the tenth house. Saturn is aspected by the fourth lord and the ninth lord of luck Mars.

Dwadashamsha

From the Moon, Rahu is in twelfth house. Rahu's dispositor Jupiter is exalted and is with the tenth lord Venus aspected by the exalted fourth lord Mars. Saturn (Ulka) is the lagna lord with the fourth lord Mars and aspected by the tenth lord Venus.

Transit

Transiting Saturn in Aquarius was aspecting the fourth house. Natal Moon, karaka for mother, in Leo was aspected

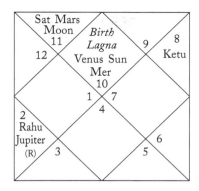

		Rahu Jupiter (R)	
Saturn Mars Moon	**Transit Chart** Jan. 24, 1966		
//Birth Lagna Venus Sun Mer			
	Ketu		

by both Saturn and Mars. Retrograde Jupiter from Aries (previous house) was also influencing the fourth house and the fourth lord.

From the natal Moon, the significator for mother, the tenth house was transited by Jupiter and aspected by Mars.

Event No. 3 :
Married to Maneka (September 23, 1974)

Sanjay met Maneka in 1973 when she was only seventeen. They developed instant liking for each other and got married a year later despite some reservations of her mother against this alliance.

Vimshottari Dasha : Moon-Mars

Birth Chart

He was running the Vimshottari dasha of Moon. Moon is the seventh lord of marriage. Sub-period lor Mars aspects the seventh house.

From Venus, the significator for marriage, the Moon aspects the fifth house of emotions. Mars, the seventh lord, aspect the fifth lord Saturn.

Note: Mars-Saturn link with the seventh house indicates that though the marriage solemnized, it did so but with some amount of tension.

Navamsha

Moon is in the seventh house and Mars is in the fifth house with the fifth lord Venus.

Yogini Dasha : Bhramari-Bhadrika (Mars-Mercury)

Birth Chart

Mars aspects the seventh house. Mercury, the ninth lord, aspects the fifth house.

From Venus, Mars is the seventh lord and Mercury is the ninth lord of luck and twelfth lord of bed pleasures.

Navamsha

Mars is in the fifth house with Venus, a natural significator for spouse and Mercury is in the ninth house.

Note: Involvement of the ninth house is also considered favourable for marriage.

From Venus, Mars is the seventh lord and Mercury, the fifth lord is placed in the fifth house.

Transit

		Ketu	Saturn
Jupiter (R)	**Transit Chart** Sept. 23, 1974		
Birth Lagna			Venus
Moon	Rahu	Mercury	Sun Mars

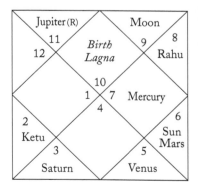

Saturn aspected the natal seventh lord, the Moon. Saturn was retrograde till February 28, 1974, so it aspected the seventh house from its previous sign Taurus. Jupiter from Aquarius in transit aspects the seventh lord, the Moon. Being retrograde it also aspects from the previous sign

Capricorn, the lagna, the natal lagna lord Saturn and the seventh house.

Event No. 4 :
Mother lost Elections (March 21, 1977)

Indira Gandhi was serving as the Prime Minister of India since 1966. In June 1975, the Allahabad High Court declared Indira Gandhi's election to the Lok Sabha in 1971 void on grounds of electoral malpractice. Her government then recommended that the President declare a state of emergency. During emergency fundamental rights of all citizens were suspended, arresting most of her opponents, and bestowing unrestricted powers on the Police to impose curfews and indefinitely detain citizens. The freedom of the press was abolished and all publications were subjected to censorship. Sanjay wielded tremendous power during the emergency without holding any Government office. It was said that during the emergency, he virtually ran India along with a coterie of his friends. In 1977, Indira Gandhi called elections to give the electorate a chance to vindicate her rule. Indira and Sanjay Gandhi both lost their seats.

Vimshottari Dasha : Moon-Jupiter

Birth Chart

The major period lord Moon is the significator for mother placed in the eighth house of hurdles/disgrace. The sub-period lord Jupiter is the twelfth lord of loss, aspecting the fourth house of the mother.

From the Moon, the significator for mother, the sub-period lord Jupiter is both the fifth and the eighth lord placed with the tenth lord of profession, Venus.

Note: Combination of the eighth and tenth houses has already been discussed for break/change in profession.

Dwadashamsha

From the Moon, the major period lord Moon is the seventh lord (killer). The sub-period lord Jupiter is the twelfth lord of losses and placed with the tenth lord Venus, giving an indication of change.

Yogini Dasha : Bhramari-Sankata (Mars-Rahu)

Birth Chart

From the Lagna, Mars (Bhramari) is the fourth lord placed in the twelfth house of losses. Rahu (Sankata) is placed in the fifth house (second to the fourth house).

Note: Rahu and Mars are mutually placed in sixth and eighth house from each other forming *shadashtaka* (6-8) position. Planets posited 6-8 or 2-12 from each other do not give favourable results in their periods.

From the Moon, Mars (Bhramari) is the fourth lord. It signifies events pertaining to the mother. It is not much afflicted. Rahu (Sankata) is in the tenth house of profession. Venus, the dispositor of Rahu is in third house with the eighth lord Jupiter.

Dwadashamsha

Mars is the fourth lord and Rahu is placed in the twelfth house. Mars and Rahu are 2-12 from each other.

From the Moon, the analysis is the same. Rahu's dispositor Jupiter is the twelfth lord, placed with the tenth lord Venus.

Transit

Saturn aspected the fourth house and the fourth lord, and natal Mars (from the previous sign). It was also afflicting the natal Moon, from its retrograde position Gemini. Transiting Mars afflicted the natal Moon. Rahu-Ketu axis was afflicting the tenth and fourth houses. So the transiting planets were concentrating on the house of mother with predominant effect of the malefics.

Mercury Sun	Ketu Venus	Jupiter	
Mars	**Transit Chart** March 21, 1977		Saturn (R)
Birth Lagna			
		Rahu	

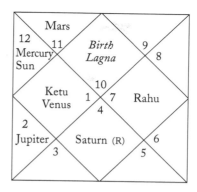

Event No. 5 :
Won Lok Sabha Elections (January 1980)

The Morarji government of 1977 which came into power after the fall of Indira Gandhi consisted of divergent, politically ambitious, elements united only in their hatred for Gandhis. The clever Indira Gandhi exploited their mutual differences and came back to power after shrewd political manipulations. Sanjay Gandhi won the next Lok Sabha elections held in January 1980.

Vimshottari Dasha : Moon-Mercury

Birth Chart

Major period lord Moon is the seventh lord placed in the eighth house.

Note : Moon being the seventh lord gives position and status. Same Moon being placed in the eighth house can cause loss of post or position, which it did anyway.

Mercury is the sixth lord placed in the eleventh house, shows victory in a fight, which is an election here. Mercury is also the ninth lord of luck, but placed with the eighth lord Sun. Involvement of eighth lord is not desirable for a long lasting victory.

Dashamsha

Moon is the eleventh lord of achievements, placed in the fourth house of Parliament and aspects the tenth house of distinction. Mercury is the tenth lord exalted in lagna.

Note: Major period and sub-period lords are placed 4-10 to each other, a favourable disposition.

Yogini Dasha : Bhadrika-Siddha (Mercury-Venus)

Birth Chart

Mercury (Bhadrika) is the sixth lord placed in the eleventh house denoting gains from elections. Venus (Siddha) is the tenth lord placed in the tenth house.

Dashamsha

Mercury is the tenth lord exalted and Venus is the ninth lord placed in the tenth house.

Note: Mercury and Venus are placed 4-10 to each other, like the Vimshottari Dasha lords.

Transit

Ketu	**Transit Chart**		
Birth Lagna Venus	January 1980		Mars (R) Jupiter(R) Rahu
Sun Mercury			Saturn (R)

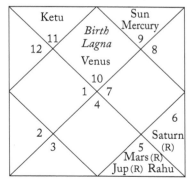

Saturn being retrograde aspects the tenth house from Leo (the previous house). Jupiter does not aspect the tenth house, but aspects the fourth house and natal fourth lord, Mars, thus activating the house of Parliament. Mars executed the orders of Saturn and Jupiter, by aspecting the tenth house, from its retrograde position, Cancer (the preceding house).

Event No. 6 :
Killed in an Air Crash (June 23, 1980)

Sanjay Gandhi died instantly from head wounds in an air crash on 23 June 1980 near Safdarjung Airport in New Delhi. He was flying a new aircraft of the Delhi Flying Club, and, while performing an aerobatic manoeuvre over his office, lost control and crashed.

Vimshottari Dasha : Moon-Mercury

Birth Chart
   Moon is the seventh lord (a killer) placed in the eighth house of sudden mishaps.
   Mercury is the sixth lord of accidents placed with the eighth lord, the Sun.
   From the Moon, Mercury is the second lord, hence a killer.

Navamsha
   The Moon is the seventh lord placed in the seventh house (a killer) and Mercury is the sixth lord aspected by the eighth lord.

Yogini Dasha : Bhadrika-Siddha (Mercury-Venus)

Birth Chart
   The role of Mercury (Bhadrika), the sixth lord, has been discussed already. Venus (Siddha) is the tenth lord placed with the twelfth lord of losses, Jupiter.
   From the Moon, Mercury is the second lord (killer), placed in the fourth house of vehicles, afflicted by Rahu-Ketu axis. Venus is the tenth lord placed with the eighth lord Jupiter.

Navamsha
   In the Navamsha chart, Mercury (Bhadrika) is the sixth

148

lord aspected by *marakesha*, the eighth lord Sun, making it more dreadful.

From the Moon, Mercury (Bhadrika) is aspected by the second lord (killer), the Sun. Venus (Siddha) is with the sixth lord Jupiter aspected by the seventh and eighth lord, Saturn, becoming a killer.

Transit

		Venus	Sun
	Transit Chart June 23, 1980		Rahu Mercury
Birth Lagna Ketu			Saturn Jupiter Mars
		Moon	

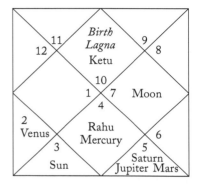

Saturn, Jupiter and Mars, all were in the eighth house of annihilation. Ketu-Rahu axis was afflicting the lagna.

Case Two: John F. Kennedy

Born on May 29, 1917, 15:01 hours (EST), Brookline, Massachusetts, USA.

John F. Kennedy, commonly referred to by his initials JFK, was an American politician who served as the 35th President of the United States from January 1961 until his assassination in November 1963. Kennedy served at the height of the Cold War, and much of his presidency focused on managing relations with the Soviet Union. A member of the Democratic Party, Kennedy represented the state of Massachusetts in the United States House of Representatives and the United States Senate prior to becoming president.

149

John F. Kennedy (Covering two cycles of Yogini Dasha)

Born on May 29, 1917, 15:01 hours (EST), Brookline, MA, USA.

	Mars Mercury	Jupiter Sun Venus	Ketu
		John F Kennedy Birth Chart	Saturn
			Moon
Rahu			Lagna

Lagna	27°28'	Mars	25°46'	Venus	24°07'
Sun	15°17'	Mercury	28°06'	Saturn	4°27'
Moon	24°30'	Jupiter	0°21'	Rahu	18°32'

Ketu		Sun	
		Navamsha (D9)	
Jupiter			Venus Saturn
Mercury	Moon Mars		Lagna Rahu

	Rahu Moon	Lagna Jupiter	
		Drekkana (D3)	Saturn
Venus			
Mercury Mars		Ketu	Sun

	Moon Saturn		Sun Rahu
Lagna	**Dashamsha (D10)**		
Jupiter Mercury			
Mars Ketu			Venus

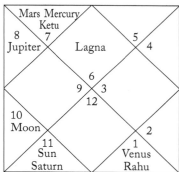

	Venus Rahu		
Sun Saturn	**Saptamsha (D7)**		
Moon			
	Jupiter	Mercury Mars Ketu	Lagna

Salient Features of the Horoscope

1. Lagna is Virgo, aspected by one malefic Saturn, which has gained all the more maleficence by being the sixth lord. Lagna lord, Mercury is with the eighth lord Mars and is aspected by another malefic Saturn.

   The Moon is in the royal sign Leo, unaspected by any benefic or malefic.

   The Sun is in its enemy's sign, that of Venus, with Venus itself. Jupiter is also posited with the Sun.

   The influence of sixth and eighth lords, Saturn and Mars, on the lagna is noticed distinctly which is a very adverse feature of this birth chart.

2. Two malefics Rahu-Ketu in the kendras (quadrants) and no benefic, do not provide much strength to the lagna.

Table of Events

	Date	Event	Vimshottari	Yogini
1.	Aug 12, 1944	Elder brother Joseph was killed	Rahu-Rahu-Sat	Bhadrika-Ulka (Mercury-Saturn)
2.	Nov 4, 1952	Became Senator	Rahu-Mercury	Ulka-Dhanya (Saturn-Jupiter)
3.	Sep 12, 1953	Got Married	Rahu-Mercury	Ulka-Bhadrika (Saturn-Mercury)
4.	Nov 27, 1957	Birth of daughter Caroline Kennedy	Rahu-Venus	Siddha-Dhanya (Venus-Jupiter)
5.	Nov 8, 1960	Became President of USA	Rahu-Mars	Siddha-Ulka (Venus-Saturn)
6.	Nov 25, 1960	Birth of son John Kennedy Jr.	Rahu-Mars	Siddha-Ulka (Venus-Saturn)
7.	Aug 9, 1963	Son died Patrick	Jupiter-Jupiter	Sankata-Pingala (Rahu-Sun)
8.	Nov 22, 1963	Was shot dead	Jupiter-Saturn-Saturn	Sankata-Dhanya (Rahu-Jupiter)

Two benefics Jupiter and Venus, in a trine, though with a cruel planet Sun, are a redeeming feature.

3. A malefic in the eleventh house is a welcome feature, especially if the malefic is the sixth lord.

4. The tenth lord in the eighth house, with the eighth lord, aspected by the fifth and sixth lord promises sudden rise and threatens sudden fall.

5. *Rajayogas*

   (a) The tenth lord is aspected by the fifth lord. A Rajayoga is being formed which gets blemished due to the involvement of sixth and eighth houses.

   (b) The fifth lord aspects the lagna and the lagna lord. This combination is also blemished by the involvement of the twelfth lord Sun.

6. *Arishta Yogas*

   (a) The lagna lord Mercury is in the eighth house with

the eighth lord Mars, aspected by the sixth lord Saturn. This is one of the most dreaded Arishta Yogas.

(b) The eighth lord Mars aspects the eleventh house – an arishta for the elder brother.

(c) The fifth lord Saturn aspected by the eighth lord Mars – an Arishta for the progeny.

Event No. 1 :
Elder Brother killed in World War II (Aug 12, 1944)

Elder brother Joseph was a United States Navy lieutenant. He was killed in action during World War II while serving as a land-based patrol bomber pilot.

Vimshottari Dasha : Rahu-Rahu

Birth Chart
Rahu is placed in the fourth house (it is the sixth from the eleventh house of elder brother).

From Jupiter, the significator for the elder brother, Rahu is placed in the eighth house.

Note: Since Rahu-Rahu period of 2yr-8m-12 days is very long, one can go upto sub-sub-period, which is of Saturn in this case. Now concentrate on Saturn:

From Lagna
(i) Saturn is the sixth lord of accidents placed in the eleventh house of elder brother.

(ii) Saturn is more fatal being aspected by the eighth lord, violent Mars.

Drekkana
From Jupiter, Rahu is in the twelfth house. Rahu's dispositor is Mars, which is the seventh lord, placed in the eighth house with second lord Mercury, becoming a qualified killer.

Note: Mars in the eighth house gives violent death.

Yogini Dasha : Bhadrika-Ulka (Mercury-Saturn)

Birth Chart

From Jupiter, Mercury (Bhadrika) is the second lord placed with the seventh lord Mars, thus it gains killing propensity. Saturn (Ulka) is in the third house of longevity aspected by the seventh lord Mars.

Note: The third house represents the mode of death, according to Parashara.

Drekkana

From Jupiter, Mercury (Bhadrika) is the second lord placed in the eighth house with the seventh lord Mars, thus it proved to be the killer. Saturn (Ulka) is again in the third house of longevity aspected by a killer Mars. Saturn (Ulka) is also aspected by the sixth lord Venus.

Transit

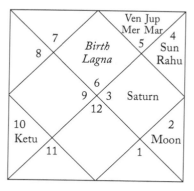

At the time of death of his brother, Saturn was in Gemini and Mars was in Leo. Thus both malefics, Mars and Saturn, the natal eighth and sixth lords, were afflicting while in transit the natal eleventh lord (elder brother) Moon in Leo. Other planets, viz., Mercury, Jupiter and Venus were also in Leo emphasizing an event pertaining to the elder brother.

The transiting Moon was in Taurus in the ninth house, eleventh from the eleventh. Additional malefic influences on the eleventh house were the Rahu-Ketu axis and the malefic twelfth lord Sun. It is obvious that all the planetary energy is concentrated on the eleventh house, the eleventh lord and, to some extent, the eleventh from the eleventh house.

Event No. 2 :
Became a Senator (November 4, 1952)

U.S. Senate elections were held on November 4, 1952. Kennedy served as the junior Senator from Massachusetts from 1953 until 1960. While serving in the Senate, he published *Profiles in Courage*, which won the Pulitzer Prize for Biography.

Vimshottari : Rahu-Mercury

Birth Chart
Rahu is in the fourth house (Senate) in Sagittarius (a royal sign). Sub-period lord Mercury is the lord of the tenth house from the lagna. Rahu and Mercury are placed in the mutually beneficial 5-9 position from each other. Mercury is also the tenth lord from the mahadasha lord Rahu, placed in the fifth house in association with a strong fifth lord.

Dashamsha
Rahu is in the fifth house of dignity associated with the royal graha Sun and aspected by the tenth lord Mars from the eleventh house of achievements. The sub-period lord Mercury, also Rahu's dispositor, associates with the eleventh lord Jupiter and gets aspected by the lagna lord Saturn. Mercury as the eighth lord in the twelfth house also forms a *Vipareeta Raja-yoga* that indicates rise in status.

Yogini Dasha : Ulka-Dhanya (Saturn-Jupiter)

Saturn as the sixth lord in the eleventh in the chart of a politician indicates success in an election. This Saturn is the lagna lord of the Dashamsha indicating rise in status. Jupiter is the fourth lord (Senate) in the auspicious ninth house, associated with the ninth lord Venus and the royal Sun. Saturn and Jupiter are placed in the mutually harmonious 3/11 position.

Transit

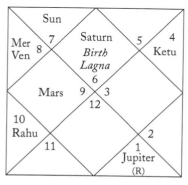

	Jupiter (R)		
	Transit Chart Nov. 4, 1952		Ketu
Rahu			
Mars	Mercury Venus	Sun	*Birth Lagna* Saturn

Saturn was in Virgo, aspecting the tenth house of distinction. Jupiter in Aries was transiting over the tenth (and lagna) lord Mercury. Mars aspected the tenth house from the fourth house Sagittarius while, from the second house, the Sun too aspected the tenth lord Mercury.

Event No. 3 :
Married to Jacqueline (September 12, 1953)

Jacqueline Bouvier met Congressman John F. Kennedy in 1952 at a dinner party. That November, he was elected as a United States Senator from Massachusetts, and the couple married in 1953. They had four children, two of whom died in infancy. As First Lady, she was known for her highly publicized restoration of the White House.

Vimshottari Dasha : Rahu-Mercury

Birth Chart

Rahu is in the fourth house. Rahu's dispositor Jupiter is the seventh lord of spouse, placed with Venus, the natural significator of marriage. Sub-period lord Mercury is the lagna lord, aspected by the fifth lord of romance, Saturn.

From Venus, Rahu's dispositor Jupiter is with Venus. Mercury is the fifth lord placed with the seventh lord Mars.

Navamsha

Rahu is placed in Navamsha lagna, aspected by the seventh lord Jupiter. Mercury is the lagna lord of Navamsha.

From Venus, Rahu is aspected by the fifth lord Jupiter. Rahu's dispositor is Mercury, which is again in the fifth house. Sub-period lord Mercury being in fifth house became responsible for the marriage.

Yogini Dasha : Ulka-Bhadrika (Saturn-Mercury)

Birth Chart

Saturn (Ulka) is the fifth lord aspecting the fifth house. Marcury (Bhadrika) is asected by the fifth lord.

From Venus, Saturn (Ulka) aspects the fifth house and the fifth lord Mercury. Mercury (Bhadrika) is the fifth lord associated with the seventh lord Mars.

Navamsha

Saturn (Ulka) is with Venus and also the seventh lord from Venus.

Mercury (Bhadrika) is the lagna lord of the Navamsha placed in the fifth house from Venus.

Note: As mentioned earlier, the lagna lord of the Navamsha chart can effect marriage.

Transit

			Jupiter
			Venus Ketu
	Transit Chart Sept. 12, 1953		
Rahu			Mars Sun
		Moon Saturn	*Birth Lagna* Mercury

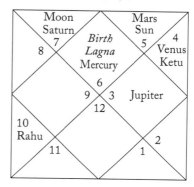

Up to August 21, 1953, Saturn was in Virgo, aspecting the seventh house. Up to August 29, 1953, Jupiter in Taurus transited over the natal seventh lord Jupiter. The permission being granted by these two planets in August itself, Mars, the commander-in-chief executed the orders, by aspecting the seventh house, in September.

Event No. 4 :
Birth of Daughter Caroline Kennedy (Nov. 27, 1957)

Caroline Bouvier Kennedy is an American author, attorney, and diplomat who served as the United States Ambassador to Japan. She is a prominent member of the Kennedy family and the only surviving child of President John F. Kennedy and First Lady Jacqueline Bouvier Kennedy.

Vimshottari Dasha : Rahu-Venus

Birth Chart

Rahu's dispositor, Jupiter, is the natural significator of progeny, aspects the fifth house of progeny. Sub-period lord Venus is with Jupiter, placed in the ninth house (an alternate house of progeny).

Saptamsha

Rahu is aspected by the fifth lord Saturn. Venus is the

ninth lord, again aspected by the fifth lord Saturn. Rahu's dispositor is Mars, who aspects the fifth house.

Yogini Dasha : Siddha-Dhanya (Venus-Jupiter)

Birth Chart

Venus (Siddha) is with Jupiter, the significator for progeny. Venus and Jupiter both are in the alternate house of progeny, the ninth house.

Saptamsha

Venus (Siddha) is the ninth lord aspected by the fifth lord Saturn. Jupiter aspects the ninth house. Jupiter's period is often a cause of childbirth.

Transit

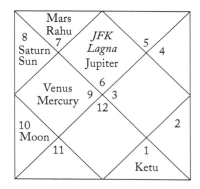

Saturn in Scorpio aspected the fifth house. Jupiter was in lagna, in Virgo, aspected the fifth house. Mars also aspected the fifth house. Moon on the day of child birth was in the fifth house. It will be interesting to note that all the three major grahas, Saturn, Jupiter and Mars, besides aspecting the fifth house, also aspected the ninth house, the alternate house for progeny. The transit of the Moon over appropriate houses generally helps in close timing of events. On the day of birth of his daughter, the Moon was transiting over the fifth house of the native.

Event No. 5 :

Became President of USA (November 8, 1960)

In the 1960 presidential election, Kennedy narrowly defeated Republican opponent Richard Nixon, who was the incumbent Vice President. At age 43, he became the youngest elected president.

Vimshottari Dasha : Rahu-Mars

Birth Chart

Rahu is in the fourth house (Senate), and Mars associates with the tenth lord aspected by the fifth lord. Mars is located in the fifth house from Rahu associating with Mercury which is the tenth lord both from the lagna and from Rahu. Rahu's dispositor, the fourth lord Jupiter, occupies the benefic ninth house in association with the ninth lord of good fortune.

From the Moon, Rahu is in the fifth house and Rahu's dispositor Jupiter is in the tenth house with the tenth lord Venus, while Mars is in its own ninth house.

Dashamsha

Rahu is in the fifth house of dignity with the Sun, the seventh lord of public life. Rahu is aspected by the tenth lord Mars, and the lagna lord Saturn and, therefore, it becomes extra-ordinarily strong.

Sub-period lord Mars is the tenth lord occupying the eleventh house of gains and achievements.

Yogini Dasha : Siddha-Ulka (Venus-Saturn)

Birth Chart

Venus (Siddha) is in the ninth house with the fourth lord Jupiter. Saturn (Ulka) is the sixth lord placed in the eleventh house, good for a political career. Saturn also aspects the tenth lord Mercury.

From the Moon, Venus (Siddha) is the tenth lord placed in the tenth house with the lagna lord Sun. (combination of lagna lord and tenth lord is a classical Rajayoga – combination of power and authority). Saturn (Ulka) is aspected by the fourth and ninth lord Mars.

Dashamsha

Venus (Siddha) is the fourth and ninth lord placed in the eighth house. Venus is in debility but at the same time, its debilitation is cancelled by the aspect of Jupiter.

Note: Debilitation of a planet is cancelled if it is aspected by the lord of a sign where this debilitated planet would be exalted. For example, in the present case, Venus in Virgo is debilitated in the Dashamsha chart. Venus is normally exalted in Pisces whose lord is Jupiter. In the present case, the debilitated Venus receives the aspect of Jupiter and thus loses its debilitation through what is known as a *Neecha-Bhanga Rajayoga*.

Saturn (Ulka) is the lord of the Dashamsha lagna.

Note: It may be noted that three planets, Jupiter, Venus and Saturn, are debilitated in the Dashamsha. Debilitated planets generally deprive the native of arrogance while cancellation of debilitation (*Neecha-Bhanga*) restores their beneficial function.

Transit

			Mars Moon
Ketu	**Transit Chart** Nov 8, 1960		
			Rahu
Saturn Jupiter	Venus	Sun Mercury	*Birth Lagna*

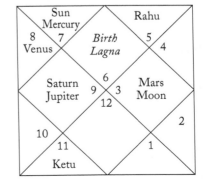

Saturn and Jupiter were in the fourth house, thus aspecting the tenth house. Mars was in the tenth house. The Moon too was in the tenth house on the day he was elected the President of USA.

Event No. 6 :
Birth of son John F. Kennedy Jr
(Born: November 25, 1960. Died: July 16, 1999)

John F. Kennedy Jr. often referred to as JFK Jr. or John John was born at Georgetown University Hospital on November 25, 1960, two weeks after his father was elected president. On July 16, 1999, Kennedy Jr. died when his airplane he was flying crashed into the Atlantic Ocean.

Vimshottari Dasha : Rahu-Mars

Birth Chart

Major period lord Rahu is in the fourth house and sub-period lord Mars is aspected by the fifth lord of progeny Saturn. Mars is in the fifth house from Rahu.

Rahu's dispositor is Jupiter, a natural significator of progeny, aspecting the fifth house.

From the Moon, Rahu is in the fifth house and Jupiter is the fifth lord.

From Jupiter, sub-period lord Mars is with the fifth lord Mercury, aspected by the ninth lord Saturn.

Saptamsha

Rahu is aspected by the fifth lord Saturn. Sub-period lord Mars aspects the fifth house.

Rahu's dispositor is again Mars, who aspects the fifth house and ninth lord Venus.

From Jupiter, Rahu is aspected by lagna lord Mars. Sub-period lord Mars aspects the Moon, the lord of ninth house (an alternate house of progeny).

Yogini Dasha : Siddha-Ulka (Venus-Saturn)

Birth Chart

Venus (Siddha) is with Jupiter. Saturn (Ulka) is the fifth lord aspecting the fifth house.

From Jupiter, Venus (Siddha) is with Jupiter and Saturn (Ulka) is the ninth lord aspecting the fifth house (as well as the ninth house) of progeny.

Saptamsha

Venus (Siddha) is the ninth lord, aspected by the fifth lord Saturn (Ulka).

From Jupiter, Siddha (Venus) aspects the lagna lord Mars. Ulka (Saturn) aspects the fifth lord, which is Jupiter itself.

Transit

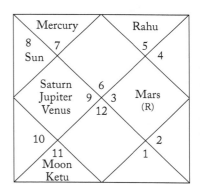

			Mars (R)
Moon Ketu	**Transit Chart** Nov. 25, 1960		
			Rahu
Saturn Jupiter Venus	Sun	Mercury	

Saturn, while being retrograde until a few months ago, aspected from its previous house Scorpio the fifth house of progeny, and the lord of the eleventh house (house of progeny for wife – fifth house *from the seventh*). Mars, from its previous house (being retrograde), and Jupiter aspected the eleventh lord, the natal Moon. Saturn from the fourth house and Mars from the tenth also aspected the fifth house from Jupiter. Saturn and Jupiter were in the fifth house from the natal Moon while Mars aspected the fifth house from the natal Moon as well as the lagna.

Event No. 7 :
Son Patrick Bouvier Kennedy died
(Born: August 7, 1963. Died: August 9, 1963)

Patrick Bouvier Kennedy was the last child of United States President John F. Kennedy and First Lady Jacqueline Bouvier Kennedy. Born prematurely, he lived just over 39 hours, putting the First Family and nation into mourning.

Indication of loss of Progeny

Birth Chart

(a) The fifth lord Saturn is in the eleventh house, aspected by the eighth lord Mars.

(b) From Jupiter, the fifth lord Mercury is with Mars, aspected by another malefic Saturn.

In Saptamsha

(c) Lagna lord Mercury is with eighth lord Mars.

(d) Fifth lord Saturn is in the sixth house with its enemy, the Sun.

(e) The significator of progeny Jupiter is in the sign of Mars, aspected by the sixth lord Saturn.

Vimshottari Dasha : Jupiter-Jupiter

Birth Chart

Jupiter, the significator of children, is very weak at 0°20' in Taurus. Jupiter is also debilitated in Navamsha.

Note : Any planet's placement in Navamsha is very important to assess its strength. A planet well placed in the birth chart, but afflicted in Navamsha, does not give favourable results.

Saptamsha

Jupiter is in the sign of Mars, aspected by the sixth lord Saturn.

Yogini Dasha : Sankata-Pingala (Rahu-Sun)

Birth Chart

Rahu (Sankata) acts as Jupiter. Jupiter is the significator of children rendered weak as shown above. Sun (Pingala) is the eighth lord from fifth house.

From Jupiter, Rahu is in the eighth house and the Sun (Pingala) along with the sixth lord Venus, afflicts Jupiter.

Note: Rahu and Sun are in 6-8 relation to each other.

Saptamsha

Rahu is in the eighth house aspected by the eighth lord Mars. The Sun is in the sixth house with the fifth (and sixth) lord Saturn. Malefic character of the Rahu-Sun period is clearly visible in the Saptamsha.

From Jupiter, Rahu is in the sixth house with Venus, the seventh lord (killer). The Sun is with the third lord of longevity, Saturn.

Transit

Jupiter Moon			Rahu
	Transit Chart August 9, 1963		Venus Sun
Saturn (R)			Mercury
Ketu			Mars

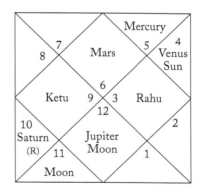

Saturn was retrograde in the fifth house, afflicting the house of progeny. Jupiter's aspect on the natal fifth lord Saturn in the eleventh house could have been useful, if it were not afflicted by transiting Saturn and Mars. Jupiter perhaps only ensured that the child was born though its affliction did not permit the survival of the newborn. The Sun was transiting over the natal fifth lord Saturn while the Moon aspected the natal lagna.

Event No. 8 :
Was shot dead (November 22, 1963)

President Kennedy was assassinated in Dallas, Texas, at 12:30 pm CST on November 22, 1963, while on a political trip to Texas. Traveling in a presidential motorcade through downtown Dallas, he was shot once in the back, the bullet exiting via his throat, and once in the head. Kennedy was taken to Hospital where he was pronounced dead 30 minutes later. He was 46 years old and had been in office for 1,036 days.

Vimshottari Dasha : Jupiter-Saturn

Birth Chart

Jupiter is the seventh lord (killer) placed with the second lord Venus (killer). Jupiter the killer is also the fourth lord of vehicles. He was shot dead while travelling by a car. Saturn is the sixth lord of accidents, aspecting the lagna lord Mercury in the eighth house. Saturn also aspects the eighth lord Mars, responsible for the violent end of life.

From the Moon, Jupiter is the eighth lord, placed with the lagna lord Sun. Saturn is the sixth and seventh lord, a killer.

Navamsha

Jupiter is the seventh lord, (killer), also debilitated. Saturn is the sixth lord placed with the second lord Venus (killer).

Note: Jupiter and Saturn are in 6-8 relation to each other.

From the Moon, Jupiter is the second lord placed in the third house of longevity. Sub-period lord Saturn is the third lord, placed with the seventh lord Venus (killer).

Yogini Dasha : Sankata-Dhanya (Rahu-Jupiter)

Birth Chart

Major period lord Rahu (Sankata) became a killer, as Rahu and Saturn have been declared unqualified killers for any lagna by Maharishi Parashara. Jupiter (Dhanya) the seventh lord placed with the second lord, proved double killer. Rahu acts as Jupiter due to disposition and, therefore, is a killer.

Navamsha

Rahu is placed in the lagna aspected by the seventh lord (killer) Jupiter. Jupiter (Dhanya) is again a killer.

Transit

Jupiter (R)			Rahu
	Transit Chart Nov. 22, 1963		
Saturn Moon			
Ketu	Mars Mercury Sun Venus		Birth Lagna

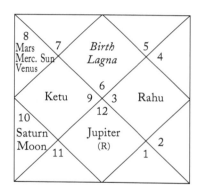

Saturn was passing over the fifth house. Jupiter was in the seventh house, retrograde, and aspected by Saturn was of no help.

Mars, was aspecting the Sun, a luminary and the twelfth lord of conspiracies.

From the Moon, Saturn was in the sixth house, Jupiter in the eighth house, and Mars in the fourth house were afflicting the lagna lord the Sun.

Note: The natal Rahu-Ketu Axis (RKA) was being transited by the RKA. Transits of natural malefics over natal malefics are always adverse when the running dasha is also adverse.

Jawaharlal Nehru (Covering three cycles of Yogini Dasha)

Born on November 14, 1889, 22:56 hours (IST), Allahabad, India.

Birth Chart (square, left)

			Rahu
			Lagna Moon
	Birth Chart		Saturn
Jupiter Ketu	Sun	Venus Mercury	Mars

Birth Chart (diamond, right)

Saturn / 6 Mars 5 / Lagna Moon / Rahu 3 / 2 / Venus Mercury 7 / 1 / 4 / 10 / 8 Sun / 9 Jupiter Ketu / 11 / 12

Lagna	22°47'	Mars	9°55'	Venus	7°15'
Sun	0°06'	Mercury	17°01'	Saturn	10°47'
Moon	17°52'	Jupiter	15°09'	Rahu	11°26'

Navamsha (D9) (square, left)

Mars Mercury			
	Navamsha (D9)		Sun Saturn Ketu
Lagna Rahu			Jupiter
Venus Moon			

Navamsha (D9) (diamond, right)

12 Mars Mercury 11 / Lagna Rahu / Venus Moon 9 / 8 / 10 / 1 / 7 / 4 Sun Saturn Ketu / 2 / 3 / 5 Jupiter / 6

Dashamsha (D10) (square, left)

Ketu Mercury		Jupiter	
	Dashamsha (D10)		Sun
			Moon Mars
Venus	Saturn	Lagna	Rahu

Dashamsha (D10) (diamond, right)

Saturn / 9 Venus 8 / Lagna / Rahu 6 / 5 Moon Mars / 10 / 7 / 4 Sun / 1 / 11 / 12 Ketu Mercury / 2 / 3 / Jupiter

Saptamsha (D7)

Jupiter		Mars Sun Moon	Lagna
Ketu			
Mercury			Rahu
	Venus	Saturn	

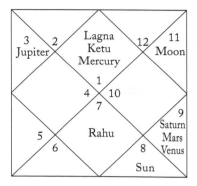

North Indian Saptamsha (D7): 5 Rahu; 4; Lagna; 2 Mars Sun Moon; 1; 3; 6; 12 Jupiter; 9; 7 Saturn; 8; 11 Ketu; Venus; 10 Mercury

Dwadashamsha (D12)

Lagna Ketu Mercury			Jupiter
Moon			
Saturn Mars Venus	Sun	Rahu	

North Indian Dwadashamsha (D12): 3 Jupiter; 2; Lagna Ketu Mercury; 12; 11 Moon; 1; 4; 10; 7; 9 Saturn Mars Venus; 5; Rahu; 6; 8; Sun

Case Three: Jawaharlal Nehru

Born on November 14, 1889, 22:56 hours (IST), Allahabad, Uttar Pradesh, India. Died May 27, 1964

Jawaharlal Nehru was the first Prime Minister of India and a central figure in Indian politics. He emerged as the paramount leader of the Indian independence movement under the tutelage of Mahatma Gandhi and ruled India from its establishment as an independent nation in 1947 until his death in 1964. He is considered to be the architect of the modern Indian nation-state: a sovereign, socialist, secular, and democratic republic. Nehru was elected by the Congress to assume office as independent India's first Prime Minister. Under Nehru's leadership, the Congress emerged as a catch-all party, dominating national and state-level politics and winning consecutive elections in 1951, 1957, and 1962. He remained popular with the people of India in spite of political troubles in his final years and failure of leadership during the 1962 Sino-Indian War.

Salient Features of the horoscope

1. Cancer lagna, with lagna lord Moon in the lagna un-aspected. The Moon lagna is the same. The Sun in a trinal house is unaspected. No involvement of the malefics with the lagna or the lagna lord gives a rare strength to the lagna.

2. An additional impetus is provided to the lagna by the placement of two benefics Venus and Mercury in the kendras (quadrants). A cruel planet Sun is in one of the trines.

3. A malefic Mars in the third house and another Ketu in the sixth house reveals the fighter hidden in the native. The native will not give up in hard times.

4. *Rajayogas*

   i) Mars, the best *yogakaraka* for the Cancer lagna, aspects the ninth and the tenth houses. This is the best of the Rajayogas present in the horoscope.

   ii) The fifth lord aspects the ninth house and the ninth lord.

   iii) The ninth lord aspects the tenth house and seventh lord. The seventh lord Saturn is also the eighth lord, the yoga is blemished.

5. *Arishta Yogas*

   i) The sixth lord Jupiter aspects the seventh lord.

   ii) The eighth lord Saturn aspects the fourth house and fourth lord.

   iii) The eighth lord aspects the eleventh house.

170

6. Special Features

    i) All the planets on one side of Rahu-Ketu Axis goes
        by the name of 'Kaala-Sarpa Yoga'. Considered an
        adverse yoga by many modern day astrologers, the
        yoga finds no mention in the important astrological
        classics.

    ii) All planets are distributed from the twelfth house
        to the sixth house, without any gap, a 'Maala Yoga'

Table of Events

	Date	Event	Vimshottari	Yogini
1.	Feb. 8, 1916	Got married	Venus-Sun	Sankata-Bhadrika (Rahu-Mercury)
2.	Nov. 19, 1917	Birth of daughter	Venus-Moon	Sankata-Ulka (Rahu-Saturn)
3.	Feb. 6, 1931	Death of father	Venus-Mercury	Bhadrika-Siddha (Mercury-Venus)
4.	Feb. 28, 1936	Death of wife	Sun-Mercury	Ulka-Siddha (Saturn-Venus)
5.	1946	Became Congress Party President	Moon-Venus	Siddha-Ulka (Venus-Saturn)
	Aug 15, 1947	Became Prime Minister	Moon-Venus	Sankata-Sankata (Rahu-Rahu)
6.	October 1962	Indo-China War, India humiliated	Rahu-Saturn	Bhramari-Ulka (Mars-Saturn)
	February 1963	Fell ill	Rahu-Saturn	Bhramari-Ulka
7.	May 27, 1964	Died	Rahu-Mercury	Bhramari-Sankata (Mars-Rahu)

Event No. 1 :
Got married (February 8, 1916)

At the age of 26 Jawaharlal Nehru married Kamla Kaul at
Delhi. Kamala was born on August 1, 1899 in a middle-class
Kashmiri Pandit family of old Delhi. She was the eldest
child of her parents and had two brothers and a sister.

Vimshottari Dasha : Venus-Sun

Birth Chart

Venus is the significator for marriage aspected by the seventh lord Saturn. Sub-period lord Sun is placed in the fifth house.

Navamsha

Venus is with the seventh lord, the Moon, and the Sun is placed in the seventh house in association with the lagna lord Saturn.

From Venus, sub-period lord Sun is the ninth lord.

Yogini Dasha : Sankata-Bhadrika (Rahu-Mercury)

Birth Chart

Rahu (Sankata) is in the twelfth house of pleasures of bed, aspected by the ninth lord Jupiter.

Rahu's dispositor Mercury, is with Venus, aspected by the seventh lord Saturn.

From Venus, Rahu is in the ninth house. Mercury is the ninth lord, placed with Venus, aspected by the fifth lord Saturn. Rahu's dispositor Mercury is placed with Venus and aspected by fifth lord Saturn.

Navamsha

Rahu is in the Navamsha lagna aspected by the lagna lord Saturn. Mercury is the ninth lord aspecting the ninth house. Rahu's dispositor Saturn is placed in the seventh house of marriage.

From Venus, Rahu is aspected by the ninth lord Sun. Mercury is the seventh lord, placed with the fifth lord Mars.

Note : It is clear from the above example how fifth, seventh and ninth houses of birth chart, and first, fifth, seventh and ninth houses of Navamsha, play predominant role in marriage making or love making periods.

Transit

Moon Jupiter Venus			Saturn (R)
	Transit Chart Feb. 8, 1916		*Birth* *Lagna* Mars(R) Ketu
Mercury Sun Rahu			

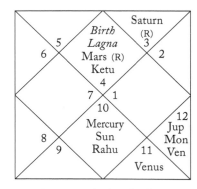

Saturn in Gemini aspects the natal seventh lord, Saturn. Till January 2, 1916, Jupiter from Aquarius, was aspecting the natal seventh lord, Saturn. Mars in Lagna aspects the seventh house.

Event No. 2 :
Birth of daughter Indira (November 19, 1917)

Kamla and Jawaharlal were blessed with a girl child, Indira Priyadarshni. Later, Indira also served as the prime minister of India. She was the first and, to date, the only female Prime Minister of India.

Vimshottari Dasha : Venus-Moon

Birth Chart

Venus is the eleventh lord (eleventh house is the fifth from the seventh house, therefore, the house of progeny for spouse). Sub-period lord Moon is the lagna lord. The birth chart does not give clear indication.

Saptamsha

Venus is the fifth lord aspected by Jupiter, the natural significator of progeny. The Moon is aspected by the fifth lord Venus.

From Jupiter, Venus is in the ninth house, aspected by the fifth lord the Moon. Sub-period lord Moon is the fifth lord.

Yogini Dasha : Sankata-Ulka (Rahu-Saturn)

Birth Chart
Rahu (Sankata) and Saturn (Ulka), both are aspected by the ninth lord, Jupiter, the child giver.

Saptamsha
Rahu aspects the ninth house and Saturn is posited in the fifth house.

From Jupiter, Rahu is aspected by the ninth lord Mars. Saturn aspects the fifth house.

Transit

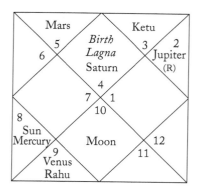

Saturn in lagna aspects the natal fifth lord Mars. Jupiter in Taurus aspects the fifth house. Mars in Leo aspects the fifth house.

Event No. 3 :
Death of father Motilal Nehru (February 6, 1931)

Motilal Nehru was an Indian lawyer, an activist of Indian Independence Movement and an important leader who also served as the Congress president twice.

Vimshottari Dasha : Venus-Mercury

Birth Chart

Venus and Mercury both are placed in the fourth house, which is eighth from the ninth house.

Ninth house as lagna of father: Major period lord Venus is the eighth lord and sub-period lord Mercury is the seventh lord (killer).

From the Sun, Venus is the seventh lord (killer) and Mercury is the eighth lord placed with the seventh lord Venus.

Yogini Dasha : Bhadrika-Siddha (Mercury-Venus)

Mercury and Venus both are the repetition of Vimshottari Dasha and have been discussed above. Here Yogini dasha confirms, what is indicated by the Vimshottari dasha.

Note: Serious students of astrology are urged to use more than one dasha systems for their predictions.

Transit

Rahu			Jupiter (R)
			Birth Lagna Mars(R)
	Transit Chart Feb. 6, 1931		
Sun			
Saturn Venus Mercury			Moon Ketu

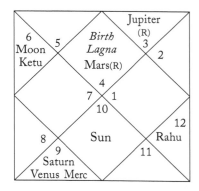

Saturn was in Sagittarius, thus transiting over the ninth lord Jupiter. Rahu-Ketu axis also afflicted the ninth house. Mars when in the previous sign, Gemini, also afflicted the natal ninth lord Jupiter. On the day of the death of his father, the Moon also aspected the ninth house.

Event No. 4 :
Death of wife Kamala Nehru (February 28, 1936)

Kamala Nehru died of pulmonary tuberculosis in Switzerland on February 28, 1936.

Vimshottari Dasha : Sun-Mercury

Birth Chart

Major period lord, the Sun, is the second lord (second house being eighth from the seventh house, hence the house for longevity of wife). Sub-period lord Mercury is the twelfth lord (sixth from the seventh house, indicating illness for the wife). Mercury is also placed with Venus, the significator of the spouse.

From Venus, the significator for spouse, the Sun is in the second house (killer). Mercury is placed with Venus.

Navamsha

Sun is the eighth lord placed in the seventh house of spouse. Mercury is the sixth lord.

From Venus, the Sun is in the eighth house with the second lord Saturn (killer). The Sun is also afflicted by the Rahu-Ketu axis. Mercury is the seventh lord (killer) debilitated and is with the twelfth lord Mars.

Yogini Dasha : Ulka-Siddha (Saturn-Venus)

Birth Chart

Saturn (Ulka) is the seventh and eighth lord placed in the second house (longevity for wife). Venus the significator of wife is afflicted by the aspect of seventh and eighth lord Saturn.

From Venus, Saturn is aspected by the sixth lord Jupiter.

Navamsha

Saturn (Ulka) is the lagna lord placed with the eighth lord, the inimical Sun. Saturn is also afflicted by the Rahu-

Ketu axis. Venus (Siddha) representing the wife is with the seventh lord the Moon (killer).

From Venus, Saturn is the second lord placed in the eighth house under the heavy affliction of Sun, Rahu and Ketu.

Note: Saturn (Ulka) and Venus (Siddha) are in 6-8 relation to each other.

Transit

Mars		Moon	Ketu
Saturn Sun	**Transit Chart** Feb. 28, 1936		Birth Lagna
Venus Mercury			
Rahu	Jupiter		

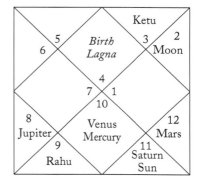

Saturn in Aquarius aspected the natal seventh lord Saturn. Mars afflicted natal Venus, the significator of spouse.

Rahu and Ketu were in 6-12 axis. It also becomes 12-6 axis for the spouse, if seventh house is taken as lagna for the spouse.

Note: Rahu was transiting over natal Ketu and Ketu was transiting over natal Rahu.

Event No. 5 :
Became Congress Party President (1946) and eventually became Prime Minister (August 15, 1947)

Nehru was elected by the Congress to assume office as independent India's first Prime Minister, although the question of leadership had been settled as far back as 1941, when Gandhi acknowledged Nehru as his political heir and successor. Despite Gandhi having made his choice known,

12 of 15 state committees nominated Patel for party president. With Gandhi wanting Nehru to be president, now the Sardar was asked to withdraw his nomination, which he did at once.

Vimshottari Dasha : Moon-Venus

Moon-Venus continued to operate from 1946 when the native was elected Congress Party President till after August 15, 1947 when he assumed the office of the Prime Minister of India.

Birth Chart

Major period lord Moon is the lagna lord placed in the lagna. Period of lagna lord is generally favourable.

Sub-period lord Venus is the fourth lord of Parliament placed in the fourth house. Venus which is also the eleventh lord of achievements, aspects the tenth house of distinction.

Note: The Moon and Venus are in favourable 4-10 relation to each other.

Dashamsha

The Moon is the tenth lord placed in the eleventh house while Venus is the lagna lord aspecting the ninth house of luck. The Moon and Venus are in favourable 5-9 relation.

Yogini Dasha :

Siddha-Ulka (Venus-Saturn) – Party President

As mentioned above, the election to the post of Party President was actually to emphasize that the native would be the future Prime Minister of Independent India.

Birth Chart

Venus as the fourth and eleventh lord has been discussed. Saturn (Ulka) as the seventh lord (public life) aspects the fourth house and the fourth lord Venus. Saturn also aspects the eleventh house of achievements.

Dashamsha

Venus (Siddha) is the Dashamsha lagna lord aspecting the ninth house.

Saturn (Ulka), the fifth lord of dignity, aspects the tenth lord of distinction, the Moon. Saturn is also aspected by the seventh lord Mars.

Yogini Dasha:

Sankata-Sankata (Rahu-Rahu) – Prime Minister

Birth Chart

At the time of assuming office of Prime Minister, the dasha was Sankata (Rahu). Rahu is aspected by the ninth lord Jupiter and its dispositor associates with the fourth lord Venus in the fourth house. From Rahu, the fourth lord (as well as th elagna lord) joins the fifth lord in the fifth house forming a potent Raja-yoga, while a strong tenth lord aspects the lagna.

Dashamsha

Rahu is aspected by two benefics, Mercury and Jupiter. From Rahu itself, the fourth lord Jupiter and its dispositor as well as the tenth lord Mercury aspect the lagna (and Rahu).

Note: Rahu's location in the twelfth house and the aspect on it of benefics, including the ninth lord, in both the rashi as well as the Dashamsha charts, indicate the acceptance of Nehru as a distinguished leader on the international arena.

Transit

On August 15, 1947, Saturn was in Cancer, in lagna, aspecting the tenth house. Jupiter was in Libra, aspecting the tenth house. Mars aspected the tenth lord, natal Mars. The Moon, on the momentous day was in the lagna. The conglomeration of five planets in the lagna brought the native great fame.

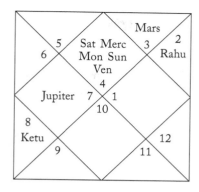

		Rahu	Mars
	Transit Chart August 15, 1947		Sat Mer Mon Sun Ven
	Ketu	Jupiter	

Event No. 6 :
India-China War : India Humiliated (October 20 - November 21, 1962), **Fell seriously ill** (February, 1963)

Sino-Indian war was a war between China and India that occurred in 1962. A disputed Himalayan border was the main pretext for war, but other issues played a role. The buildup and offensive from China occurred concurrently with the 13-day Cuban Missile Crisis (October 16-28, 1962) that saw both the United States and the Soviet Union confronting each other, and India did not receive assistance from either of these world powers until the Cuban Missile Crisis was resolved. The betrayal by China left Nehru with his reputation besmeared and his confidence shattered.

Vimshottari Dasha : Rahu-Saturn

Birth Chart

Rahu is in the twelfth house, aspected by the sixth lord Jupiter representing fights, disputes, illness, etc. In this case, sub-period lord Saturn is the seventh lord (killer) and placed in the second house is a double killer. Such dasha was bound to prove disastrous.

From the Moon, analysis is same as the lagna and the Moon lagna coincide.

Dashamsha

Rahu is in the twelfth house, aspected by the sixth lord Jupiter from the eighth house. Saturn, the sub-period lord is also aspected by the sixth lord Jupiter. The sixth house becoming prominent in this period, the war became inevitable.

Navamsha

Rahu and Saturn form 1-7 Axis in lagna, thus afflicting it along with the eighth lord Sun.

Yogini Dasha : Bhramari-Ulka (Mars-Saturn)

Birth Chart

Mars (Bhramari) is the tenth lord placed in the third house, aspects the sixth house of fights or disputes. Saturn (Ulka) is also aspected by the sixth lord Jupiter.

Dashamsha

Mars is with the tenth lord Moon, afflicted by the aspect of Saturn. Saturn is also aspected by the sixth lord Jupiter, placed in the eighth house.

This Mars-Saturn connection indicates an impending tense period.

Navamsha

Mars is with the sixth lord Mercury. Saturn is the lagna and the second lord placed with the eighth lord Sun.

From the Moon, Mars is the twelfth lord placed with the seventh lord (killer) Mercury. Saturn is the second lord (killer) placed in the eighth house.

Note: Killer planets give painful experiences in their periods, if the time of death has not come yet.

Transit

The Moon is the significator of mind. In any painful experiences giving period, an affliction to the Moon is obvious. In this case, natal Moon in Cancer lagna was

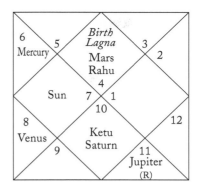

Jupiter (R)	**Transit Chart** Oct. 20, 1962		*Birth Lagna* Mars Rahu
Ketu Saturn			
	Venus	Sun	Mercury

afflicted to the maximum by the aspect of Saturn, Ketu, Rahu and Mars. No relief was available from Jupiter, who was in the eighth house.

Note: The destiny of a nation is reflected in the destiny of its great leaders.

Event No. 7 :
Died (May 27, 1964)

Nehru's health began declining steadily after 1962, and he spent months recuperating in Kashmir through 1963. Some historians attribute this dramatic decline to his surprise and chagrin over the Sino-Indian War, which he perceived as a betrayal of trust.

Vimshottari Dasha : Rahu-Mercury

Birth Chart

Rahu is in the twelfth house, aspected by the sixth lord Jupiter. Mercury is the third and twelfth lord, aspected by the seventh lord (killer) Saturn.

Note: Remember that in the absence of other killer operable, third, sixth and eleventh lords assume the role of killers.

Sub-period lord Mercury is also the third lord of longevity.

182

Navamsha

Rahu is in lagna aspected by the seventh lord (killer) Saturn and eighth lord Sun.

Note: Rahu, if aspected by the malefics, assumes the role of malefics.

Yogini Dasha : Bhramari-Sankata (Mars-Rahu)

Birth Chart

Bhramari (Mars) is in the third house of longevity, aspecting the sixth house and sixth lord Jupiter (Nehru died of sickness). Rahu is in the twelfth house, aspected by the sixth lord Jupiter.

Note: Rahu in the twelfth house qualifies to be a killer. According to Maharishi Parashara Saturn and Rahu can be unqualified killers for any lagna.

Navamsha

Mars is again in the third house of longevity, with the sixth lord of sickness, Mercury. Mars (Bhramari) aspects the sixth house also. Rahu's role as a killer has been discussed under Vimshottari dasha.

Transit

Saturn in the eighth house from lagna, aspecting the natal Sun, proved disastrous. Mars was aspecting the natal Moon.

	Jupiter Mars Mercury	Sun	Venus Rahu
Saturn	**Transit Chart** May 27, 1964		*Birth Lagna*
Ketu	Moon		

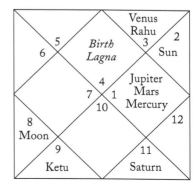

CHAPTER TWELVE

YOGINI DASHA AND THE ANNUAL CHART

The Varshaphala chart or more popularly known as the Annual Chart is the solar return chart for a native. When the Sun in transit attains the same longitude as the natal Sun in a person's horoscope, it is the beginning of a new year for the native. A chart prepared for that moment is considered to be valid for the whole year and indicates the likely events during the year.

Vimshottari and Yogini are the two dashas applied on the annual chart and are valid for a span of one year only.

For a detailed exposition and calculation of Annual chart, readers are advised to study *A Textbook of Varshaphala* by Dr. K S Charak. The method of calculation of Yogini dasha for annual chart is reproduced here from this book.

The Yogini Dasha

To the sum of the birth nakshatra and the completed years of life, add three. Divide the total by eight. The remainder gives the Yogini dasha at the commencement of the year as follows:

Remainder	Yogini Dasha	Remainder	Yogini Dasha
1	Mangala	5	Bhadrika
2	Pingala	6	Ulka
3	Dhanya	7	Siddha
4	Bhramari	8 or 0	Sankata

Calculation of Yogini Dasha for Annual Chart

Let us take up for our calculation the example of a native born on Jenuary 21, 1968 at 4:17 hours in Delhi. To calculate the Yogini dasha for the 27th year (26 completed years) for the above example chart:

(Completed years 26 + Birth nakshatra 13 + 3) ÷ 8
= 42 ÷ 8; Q = 5; R = 2.

Thus we get a quotient of 5, which is to be ignored, and a remainder of 2, which shows that the first dasha in the year will be Pingala.

Lords of Yogini Dashas and their Duration in Annual Chart

The above-mentioned eight Yogini dashas are ruled by their lords. These, along with the duration of these dashas in Annual chart are tabulated in Table XII-1.

Table XII-1

	The Yogini Dasha	Lord	Duration (days)
1.	Mangala	Moon	10
2.	Pingala	Sun	20
3.	Dhanya	Jupiter	30
4.	Bhramari	Mars	40
5.	Bhadrika	Mercury	50
6.	Ulka	Saturn	60
7.	Siddha	Venus	70
8.	Sankata	Rahu	80

The formula of calculation of balance of Yogini dasha for Annual chart is the same as for the birth chart as explained in Chapter II (page 9); but the periods of Yogini dasha for Annual chart should be used.

Example Chart

Rahu Saturn		
Mars	**Birth Chart** Jan. 21, 1968 4:17 a.m. Delhi	
Sun Mercury		Jupiter
	Lagna Venus	Moon 12°21 Ketu

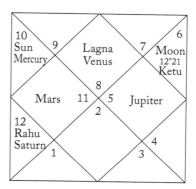

In the Example chart, where we have seen that the Pingala dasha operates at the time of the commencement of the year, the balance of Pingala dasha can be determined from the untraversed part of the Moon's nakshatra at birth. The formula for this is:

$$\frac{\text{Duration of Yogini for Annual chart} \times \text{The un-traversed portion of the Moon's nakshatra at birth}}{13°20'}$$

(Total duration of Pingala, i.e., 20 days × The un-traversed portion of the Moon's nakshatra at birth, i.e., 10°59' in our case) ÷ the total duration of a nakshatra, i.e., 13°20'.

This gives us a value of 16 days. Thus the year starts with a Bhramari balance of 16 days, the remaining 4 days, will operate towards the end of the year.

The Yogini dasha periods for the native, for his twenty-seventh year starting from January 26, 1994 are shown in table XII-2.

186

Table XII-2

	Yogini Dasha	Duration m	d	Upto d	m	y
1.	Pingala	0	16	12	2	94
2.	Dhanya	1	00	12	3	94
3.	Bhramari	1	10	22	4	94
4.	Bhadrika	1	20	12	6	94
5.	Ulka	2	0	12	8	94
6.	Siddha	2	10	22	10	94
7.	Sankata	2	20	12	1	95
8.	Mangala	0	10	22	1	95
9.	Pingala	0	04	26	1	95

The sub-periods in the Yogini dasha may also be worked out proportionately.

Method of Interpretation of Yogini Dasha in Annual Chart

Yogini Dasha for Annual Chart is to be applied in the same manner as any dasha system is applied to the birth chart.

The Yoginis, alternatively benefic and malefic, are to be interpreted by their literal meaning and by the extended application of the principles of interpretation like the lordship of Yogini, its placement in a house, its conjunction with other Yoginis, aspect of the Yoginis, etc. This method has been used throughout the book and we propose to extend the same to the Annual Charts.

Four examples which have been discussed in detail in the previous chapters have been picked up for the application of Yogini dasha on the annual charts of these examples. The fifth example is of Rajiv Gandhi for his 41st year when he became the Prime Minister of India when his mother was assasinated.

Case One :
Scholastic Achievement
(*Refer Case Study 1, page 82*)

	Lagna	Moon	Jupiter
	Annual Chart for the 27th year		Ketu
Rahu Sun			
Saturn Mars Mer Ven			

Lagna	26°46'	Mars	10°11'	Venus (R)	27°36'
Sun	22°11'	Mercury	26°14'	Saturn	25°50'
Moon	11°8'	Jupiter	7°48'	Rahu	22°46'

The girl was choosen for a scholarship which earned her a foreign trip and a training session abroad. She was running Sankata (Rahu) at that time. Now analyse Rahu in the Annual Chart.

i) Rahu (Sankata) is in the 10th house of distinction. Rahu is also with the Sun, the 5th lord of education.

The native, rightly, earned the achievement, which was also educational in nature (5th lord).

Note: A link between the fifth house and the tenth house in a natal chart tends to indicate professional education (education related to career).

ii) Rahu's dispositor is Saturn, which is the also 11th lord of monetary gains, placed in the 9th house of luck.

iii) The 9th house of luck of the Birth Chart has become the lagna for the annual chart. This is an indication that the 27th years is going to be lucky for the native.

Case Two :
Abduction (*Refer Case Study 4, page 86*)

		Moon	Jupiter (R)
	Annual Chart for the 47th year	Lagna Ketu	
Venus Rahu			
Saturn Mercury	Sun Mars		

Lagna	10°28'	Mars	8°58'	Venus	7°10'
Sun	26°12'	Mercury	0°00'	Saturn	19°34'
Moon	11°43'	Jupiter (R)	14°9'	Rahu	24°30'

The native a Tea Estate Manager was kidnapped in his 47th year. He was running Sankata (Rahu) at that time.

i) Rahu is in the 7th house placed with the 4th lord of residence, Venus. Thus affliction to the 4th house is indicated.

ii) Rahu's dispositor, Saturn, is placed in the 6th house of enemies aspected by the 6th lord retrograde Jupiter from the 12th house of imprisonment.

iii) Saturn is with Mercury, the 12th lord of confinement.

iv) Saturn is further afflicted by an intense Papakartari yoga, being placed between malefics Sun and Mars on the one side and a retrograde Rahu on the other, causing its virtual strangulation.

v) Please note that all malefics (the Sun, Mars, Saturn, Rahu-Ketu axis) in the annual chart (i.e., the transiting malefics) influence similar malefics in the natal chart by association or aspect.

Case Three :

Cancer (*Refer Case Study 9, page 78*)

	Moon	Ketu Mars
Saturn (R)	**Annual Chart for the 59th year**	Sun
Rahu	Lagna	Mercury Jupiter Venus

Lagna	12°43'	Mars	8°21'	Venus	25°02'
Sun	29°38'	Mercury	0°21'	Saturn (R)	18°18'
Moon	14°04'	Jupiter	0°58'	Rahu	2°19'

The annual chart for 59th year of native is given above.

The native suffering from cancer of rectum was operated upon in the period of Dhanya (Jupiter).

i) Jupiter is 6th lord of disease placed in the 12th house of hospitalisation with the 12th lord Mercury. The debilitated lagna lord Venus also joins Jupiter.

ii) The aspect of Mars (significator of surgery) is indicative of the surgical treatment given to the native.

iii) The seventh house represents the rectum. Its lord Mars is afflicted by the Rahu-Ketu axis.

iv) Saturn, the karaka for the rectum, is retrograde and afflicted too, by the aspect of Mars.

v) Though the lagna lord Venus is debilitated but is with exalted Mercury, causing Neecha Bhanga Raja Yoga (cancellation of debilitation). The native was saved inspite of heavy odds against him.

Case Four :
Marriage of a girl
(*Refer Case Study 2, page 72*)

		Ketu	Saturn
Lagna Jupiter (R)	**Annual Chart for the 19th year**		Venus
			Mars Sun Mercury
Moon	Rahu		

North Indian chart:
- 12, 1 : Lagna, Jupiter (R)
- 10 : Moon
- 9 : Moon
- Ketu, 2, 11, 8 : Rahu
- 5
- 3 Saturn
- Mars Sun Mercury
- 7
- 4, 6
- Venus

Lagna	12°05'	Mars	25°08'	Venus	20°00'
Sun	9°00'	Mercury	17°10'	Saturn	21°40'
Moon	7°21'	Jupiter (R)	20°04'	Rahu	22°11'

The annual chart for the 19th year of native is given here.

The native got married in her 19th year, when she was running Yogini Dasha of Pingala (Sun) in her annual chart.

i)   The Sun is the 7th lord placed in 7th house of annual chart.

ii) The Sun is also placed with the 5th lord of emotions, Mercury, showing a case of love marriage.

Case Five :
Rise to Power (*Rajiv Gandhi*)

This example is of Mr. Rajiv Gandhi, who in his 41st year became the strongest ever Prime Minister of India after the assasination of his mother.

The native ascended to power in the Yogini dasha of Siddha (Venus). Now analyse the Annual Chart.

Birth Chart
Aug. 20, 1944
7:11 a.m.
Bombay
Sunday

			Saturn
	Birth Chart Aug. 20, 1944 7:11 a.m. Bombay Sunday		Rahu
Ketu			Lagna Sun Jup Mon 17°8' Mer Ven
			Mars

		Moon Rahu	
	Annual Chart for the 41st year		
			Sun Mer (R) Venus
Jupiter (R)	Lagna Mars Ketu	Saturn	

Lagna	9°26'	Mars	7°42'	Venus	21°45'
Sun	3°50'	Mercury (R)	18°20'	Saturn	17°13'
Moon	9°40'	Jupiter (R)	9°38'	Rahu	8°55'

i) Venus (Siddha) is the 7th lord (giver of position) placed in the 10th house of distinction in the royal sign Leo.

ii) Venus (Siddha) is also aspected by the 5th lord Jupiter, which confers dignity.

iii) Association of the retrograde eighth lord Mercury indicates the tragedy which preceeded his sudden rise to power.

CHAPTER THIRTEEN

DERIVED MEANINGS OF THE YOGINIS[1]

The nomenclature chosen by the classical writers reveals some significant meanings[2] and when interpreted they seem to throw sigfnificant light on interpretation of the Yogini dasha. This further clarifies the characteristics and nature of that particular situation or the personality.

The names of the eight Yoginis are Mangala, Pingala, Dhanya, Bhramari, Bhadrika, Ulka, Siddha and Sankata governed respectively by Moon, Sun, Jupiter, Mars, Mercury, Saturn, Venus and Rahu (Ketu). The benefic and malefic planets are positioned alternatively and hence the dasha period of good and bad comes alternatively which reminds us of the age-old dictum:

"चक्रवत्परिवर्तन्ते सुखानि दुःखानिच"

Such situations do prepare us to face good and bad with equanimity as revealed in the Bhagavadgita while describing the path of a *sthitaprajna*.

"दुःखेष्वनुद्विग्नमनः सुखेषु विगतस्पृहः"

Out of the total thirty six years of the Yogini dasha in the life span of a native the good results cover only sixteen

---

1. This paper was contributed by Late Dr. (Mrs.) Ratnam Nilakantan, Jyotish Visharad, Reader in Sanskrit, University of Delhi.

2. The dictionaries utilised (a) Sanskrit-Eng. dictionary, Monie Williams; (b) Sabda Kalpadruma

years while the bad ones cover twenty years. This bitter truth gives strength to bear with the difficulties and take advantage of the good periods of one's life.

A chart produced in the following pages shows the different meanings attached to each nomenclature and the interpretation arrived at on the basis of their meanings. It is for the researchers in Astrology to find whether this type of interpretation would help in the application of Yogini dasha in a particular horoscope. This has to be put through the test of experimentation and application.

The notable points in the interpretative analysis are as under.

1. The period of Mangala of one year belonging to the Moon has to offer only good results and this leads us to conclude that during this period the native will have only benefic effects, though the percentage of result will very much depend upon the position of the Moon in the natal chart.

2. The two year period of the Sun, Pingala, the second dasha has the mixed results where benefic results seems to be more pronounced than the malefic.

3. The third period of Dhanya is that of Jupiter and it extends for three years. We naturally expect only benefic results during this period. Surprisingly one meaning leads to the interpretation of being an atheist. In such a case it is quite possible that Jupiter is very highly afflicted.

4. Bhramari, the fourth period of four years is that of Mars and this period also has the mixed results of both benefic and malefic nature.

5. Bhadrika, the fifth period of five years of Mercury, as the very name reveals, gives only benefic results.

6. Saturn rules over the sixth period of six years called Ulka. It has one or two benefic results also to its credit.

7. Siddha, of Venus, is the giver of all success and accomplishments. A study of these seven years reveals that the beneficence bestowed by the preceptor of demons is much more than the other benefic planets.

8. The last period of eight years of Sankata is that of Rahu-Ketu. All that is hard, difficult and painstaking belongs to this period. There is one meaning which refers to a particular goddess by the name in Benaras which may indicate some divine grace that may befall the person. Is it due to Ketu, the planet of emancipation and the bestower of the highest knowledge?

Meanings	Extended meaning (interpretation)
Mangala (Moon)	
1. A faithful wife (पतिव्रता)	1. Will get a faithful wife, wife will be faithful.
2. Auspicious	2. An auspicious form, will bring good result.
3. Lucky (lucky issues)	3. Brings luck, children, will be fortunate, lucky period for children.
4. Gold	4. Some good wealth is assured, will shine best, some good and meritorious recognition.
5. Sandalwood	5. Will have soothing effect on others, will cure the distress and pain, goodness and greatness will spread every where all round him.
6. A good omen auspicious moment	6. An auspicious time, a good time, a good turn of event.
7. Prayer, benediction, amulet	7. Will be protected from dangers, evil, and mis-happenings. Some one else may protect him.
8. A festival, solemn ceremony, important occasion	8. Some solemn ceremony may take place in the household, some important occasion may arise, will take part in a ceremony or a festival.
9. A good old custom	9. Will stick to the traditional path, old custom.

Meanings	Extended meaning (*interpretation*)
10. The smell of Jasmine	10. His beneficence and goodness will spread in the neighbourhood. Everyone will realise his greatness.
11. The white and blue flowering durva grass (शुक्रदुर्वा, नीलदुर्वा)	11. Will create a congenial, peaceful, harmonious and religious atmosphere.
12. Parvati (पार्वती)	12. Will reach an esteemed position.
13. Turmeric power (हरिद्रा)	13. Will have the healing effect, will create an auspicious atmosphere.
14. The tree '*Polgamia Glabra*' used medicinally (करंजभेद)	14. Will be successful in the remedial measure, will be cured of the disease, will cure others, sorrows, defects and ailments.
15. Name of the Capital of Udayana	15. Significant and important place is achieved.
16. Name of Agni (*Grihyas*)	16. Achieve an important position, steadfast in his attitude and approach, keep himself pure and steady inspite of odd circumstances.
17. Name of the planet Mars	17. Some valorous deed will be done.
18. Name of a king belonging to the race of Manu	18. Will reach a highly prestigious, respectable, noteworthy and important position.

Pingala (Sun)

1. Fire	1. Accidents due to fire; unapproachable, meeting with a fiery personality, tense, fiery and warm atmosphere created.
2. Owl	2. Will be able to take up a wise decision, will be vigilant, should be vigilant, active work which needs vigilant approach and wise decision will be undertaken.
3. An attendant of the Sun, of Rudra, of Shiva, of a Yaksha, of a danava, of a Naga or a Serpent demon, of several demons, of several ancient sages	3. Will be with the superior authority always and will carry out his orders & work well. Hence will get the appreciation of his superiors.

Meanings	Extended meaning (interpretation)
4. One of Kuber's treasures. (Name of a treasure).	4. Great money from some treasure, (hidden hereditary property)
5. Brass	5. Needs someone's help to show his greatness or capacity. Cannot shine on his own, though he has the potential.
6. Monkey	6. Will be roaming around, will not have a fixed abode, will know all the tricks of the trade.
7. Snake	7. Danger from some unexpected source, sudden danger, will be able to drive away the enemies or the tormentors.
8. Reddish brown, tannery	8. A very heated atmosphere created, will have to receive some blemish, accused, suspicion may arise against him.
9. Yellow, gold coloured	9. Very happy incident or an auspicious incident may take place, will be happy and will make others happy, congenial atmosphere created.
10. A small kind of lizard	10. An opportune moment to get the mission fulfilled, wait for an opportune moment.
11. A particular vegetable poison	11. An unknown enemy among relatives, close associates or friends, should beware of that type of enemy.
12. The 51st year in the 60 year-cycle of Jupiter	12. A very important phase in the life of a nation and individual's life leading to beneficence.
13. A species of a bird (A special kind of bird)	13. Will roam about all places as he likes, will get freedom from bondage.
14. A particular vessel of the body (the right of 3 tubular vesselswhich according to the yoga philosophy are the chief passages for breath and air – (नाड़ी विशेषः)	14. Onset of some disease connected with the heart mainly, some of the main sources of life, an important position of place, may get some relief from some type of cardiac trouble.

Meanings	*Extended meaning* (*interpretation*)
15. A kind of yellow pigment.	15. Occurrence of good or auspicious event, a very soothing occasion.
16. Yellow pigment (mineral, trisulfide of arsenic-used as yellow dye)	16. Will contact some auspicious person; or a personality poisonous in nature will get mingled with such a person.
17. Heart pea.	17. Relief from heart trouble.
18. A special kind of tree called (शिंशपा-वृक्ष) Dalbergia sissoo the Aksoha tree	18. A period in which shelter will be given to many; help others out of their troubles, will extend a soothing and helping hand to others.
19. Name of Shiva or a kindred being	19. Will do a kind act.
20. Name of a people	20. Will meet some unknown public figure.
21. Name of Lakshmi	21. Period of gain, monetary gain, financial assistance received.
22. Name of a courtesan who became remarkable for her piety	22. Association with a good and noble prostitute, pious by nature.
23. Name of a female elephant of South quarter	23. One female member of great valour and strength, will protect; will have to face a powerful female member.
24. Name of an astrological house or a period	24. A significant event may occur.
25. Name of a particular metal	25. A strong period is indicated; will overcome the obstacles, will show strength in times of need.

Dhanya (Jupiter)

1. Grains	1. Period of increase in grains.
2. Wealth in rice and grains	2. Increase in the agricultural products, the field products.
3. Bringing or bestowing wealth, opulence, rich treasure, wealth	3. Period of prosperity, increase in wealth without much labour, wealth from some unknown and unexpected source.
4. Happy	4. Family happiness will increase.
5. Auspicious, good, virtuous	5. Virtuous, auspicious and good deeds are done during this period, virtuous and auspicious occasion.

Meanings	*Extended meaning (interpretation)*
6. Wholesome, healthy	6. A healthy period, freedom from illness and health restored.
7. Infidel (disbeliever in religion), Atheist	7. Begins to disbelieve in religion; engages in anti-religious activities.
8. A spell for using or restraining magical weapons	8. Will take part in war, will get some protection from the enemy attack.
9. Corcarider	9. Enhances the status of the family by his deeds.
10. Name of a man of the vaisyas in the Krauncha dvipa	10. May have some commercial contact with some person of the commercial community in a foreign place.
11. A nurse	11. Keeps someone who is hospitalized morally and physically.
12. Name of Dhruva's wife	12. Period to attain an important position.

The quality of Dhanya

Meanings	*Extended meaning (interpretation)*
13. Sweetness (मधुरत्वम्)	13. Happy atmosphere created.
14. Coolness (शीतलत्वम्)	14. Tensions and heated atmosphere come to an end.
15. Astringent (कषायत्वम्)	15. Will face some unsavoury incidents which will prove beneficial.
16. Removes diseases like fever, cough, thirst, cold, congestion of chest, indigestion, etc.	16. All types of disease will be cured during this period.
17. Glossy, oily, moist, (स्निग्धत्वम्)	17. Will live in a kind and congenial surroundings.
18. Harsh (कटुत्वम्)	18. Very harsh experiences will be experienced.
19. Thirst (तृष्यत्वम्)	19. Thirst to achieve something.
20. Lightness (लघुत्वम्)	20. Even tension-loaded atmosphere will become lighter.
21. Belonging to urine (मूत्रलत्वम्)	21. Period of urinary trouble, free from urine trouble.
22. Pungent (तिक्त्वम्) strong scented (कटुत्वम्)	22. Will get all types of experiences with different types of people.
23. Digestive (पाचनत्वम्)	23. Will be able to withstand all troubles.
24. Attractive (रोचनत्वम्)	24. Will attract everyone by his attitude, will be good to others.

Meanings	Extended meaning (interpretation)
25. Tasty (स्वादुपाकित्वम्)	25. Will have an occasion to taste good foods.
26. Removes all maladies of fever, breath, etc. (त्रिदोषदाहश्वासामर्श-कृमिनाशित्वञ्च)	26. Will be cured of viral fever and infections.
27. Removes bile complaint (पित्तहर)	27. Removes bile complaint.

Bhramari (Mars)

1. Roving in all directions, wandering, roaming about, moving, nothing turning around	1. Will wander everywhere without any goal, move out of his own place to roam around and will come back home once in a while.
2. A whiling flame	2. Will have to face a very forceful and dangerous situation, involvement in a great fire.
3. A whirlpool	3. May get entangled in a very difficult situation from which it is hard to get out.
4. A spring, a fountain	4. People around him will shower their grace and beneficience, will have an occasion to share to give with everyone.
5. Water course	5. Will be helpful to all, will be a life saviour.
6. Giddiness, dizziness confusion, perplexity	6. State of confusion, unable to take a proper decision, mental depression leading to unsteadiness.
7. Error, mistake	7. Others will find fault with him, will be mistaken.
8. Governess (पुत्रदात्री)	8. Child will be protected or taken care of by some old lady.
9. Lac, gum (जतुक)	9. Gets attached to or adhered to things or persons.
10. A bee (षत्पदी)	10. Will hover around to collect the best that is available around him, earn more and save for the future.

Meanings	Extended meaning (interpretation)

Bhadrika (Mercury)

1. 2nd, 7th and 12th day of a lunar fortnight
1. These three days will produce benefic results and are good to start any work.

2. Celestial Ganges
2. Auspicious occasion, will meet an auspicious, pious and noble personality who will confer his blessings on him.

3. An amulet.
3. Some one else will extend a protective hand in times of need.

4. Good, brave, handsome beautiful
4. Health and dour will increase, may meet a person handsome, brave and young.

5. A kind of beam
5. Will become healthy due to nutritive food.

6. A particular pastime in sitting
6. Good period to do yoga practices

7. A kind of metre
7. Poetic talents will be revealed.

8. Life saviour (जीवन्ती)
8. Will be saved from danger, will save someone from danger.

9. Not vulnerable (अपराजिता)
9. Will even be victorious, no one can win over him, will face success everywhere.

10. Name of a people
10. Will come into contact with common people

11. Name of a prince
11. Will meet a person in high position, will get right contacts.

Ulka (Saturn)

1. A fiery phenomenon in the sky, a meteor, fire falling from heaven
1. A great calamity will befall the family, on the person, on the land, on the country where he lives.

2. Flame, a fire brand (अग्निशिखा), a torch
2. Some accident due to fire.

3. Dry grain, etc., set on fire
3. Some danger due to fire which will destroy each and everything.

4. One of the principal dashas or aspect of planets indicating the fate of men
4. Indication of a bad time.

5. Jyotisha (astrology)
5. Inclination to learn Jyotish.

Meanings	*Extended meaning (interpretation)*
6. Name of grammer	6. Will have an occasion to show his talents in language, will be able to express better.
7. When Ulka falls time indicates danger to the country and the king	7. Time of danger for the family and the nation.

Siddha (Venus)

1. To gain, to accomplish, to succeed, fulfilled.	1. Period of success in all walks of life, gainful period, will accomplish his goal and ambition.
2. To become famous, illustrious	2. Becomes famous.
3. To command	3. Holds a commanding position in office.
4. To instruct	4. Will be a successful instructor.
5. To acquire	5. Will acquire according to his wish.
6. One who has attained the highest object	6. Mission will be fulfilled.
7. Thoroughly skilled or well versed	7. Will become skilled or well-versed in the field undertaken.
8. Beautified	8. Will become robust, healthy and beautiful.
9. Enclosed with supernatural faculties, divine, holy personage, great saint, one who has attained the status of beatitude	9. Period of super human power, more powerful mentally and physically, will come across a high personage, will have a philosophical bent of mind and can reach the highest status.
10. Sacred, holy	10. Will be respected by all for his good qualities.
11. Setting a target	11. Period of concentration to achieve his goal.
12. Cooked	12. Will reach a well groomed stage.
13. Dressed	13. Ready to do any errand or to go out anywhere.
14. Healed, cured	14. Will be cured of the ailment.
15. Valid, admitted to be true or right, established, proved	15. Validity of statement made, will be proclaimed, opinion is admitted as true and valid.

Meanings	Extended meaning (interpretation)
16. Adjudicated	16. Adjustment between the two warring parties.
17. Decided	17. Will be able to take proper decision.
18. Liquidated, terminated	18. Terminated from the present position
19. Paid, settled	19. Problem solved or settled.
20. Well known, notorious, celebrated	20. Will become a celebrity.
21. Effective, powerful	21. Will become effective and powerful in his endeavours.
22. Miraculous	22. Sudden happenings.
23. Subdued, brought into subjection	23. Forced to come under subjection.
24. Obedient	24. Will carry out orders implicitly.
25. Peculiar	25. Special occasion.
26. Invariable, unalterable	26. Rigid in attitude, not-willing to change his ideas and ideals, sticks to his own views, and ideas.
27. A great adept in music	27. Advancement in music.
28. The 21st of the astrological yogas	28. Reach a Yogic stage.
29. A law suit, judicial	29. Enter into a law suit.
30. Name of a deva gandharva	30. Will be good in music, will be known in the field of music.
31. Name of a Rajarshi	31. Will remain unperturbed even during difficult situations.
32. Name of a king	32. Will attain an important position.
33. Name of a Brahmin	33. Will be respected for his scholarship.
34. Name of an author	34. Will be a good will writer. Write a book, publish a book.
35. A kind of thorn apple or a kind of plant	35. Will have to take a hard decision, though it hurts others but ultimately will turn out to be good.
36. A sort of hard sugar	36. Sweet outcome after a period of struggle.
37. A siddha or a semi divine female	37. Will meet a highly spiritual lady.
38. One of the yoginis	38. Reaches a special respectable state.
39. A kind of a medicinal plant	39. Ailment will be cured.

Meanings	*Extended meaning* (*interpretation*)
40. A kind of a root	40. Will take the role of a foundation stone of the family.
41. Sea salt	41. Will be recognised as an important person in life where due recognition is given.

Sankata (Rahu-Ketu)

1. Impervious (not affording passage to argument)	1. Will act according to own decision without listening to any one's advise.
2. Impassable, dangerous	2. Dangerous, very difficult period.
3. Crowded (with)	3. Surrounded by people.
4. Contracted	4. Defamed, meeting *narrow minded* or mean people.
5. A difficulty	5. Facing a difficult situation.
6. Risk	6. Can take a risk to achieve the end, face a risky situation.
7. Danger to or from	7. Will face some danger or will cause danger.
8. Closed	8. Path of success will be closed.
9. Brought together	9. Estranged persons will be brought together.
10. Dense	10. A hard period, may not be in a position to finish the work in hand.
11. Critical	11. All his work and atitude will be criticised.
12. Name of a particular person	12. Meets a new personality.
13. Name of a species of flamingo	13. Will fly away one day from his native place.
14. A narrow passage	14. Difficult period to reach the goal or target.
15. Defile, make dirty, pollute, ceremonially unclean	15. Will engage in dirty and hazardous deeds, unclean work.
16. Difficulty	16. Will face difficulties.
17. A strait (narrow, limited)	17. Will follow a narrow or a crooked path.
18. Name of a goddess workshipped in Benaras	18. Will have the strength and power to remove difficulties. Some divine grace will be bestowed.
19. A type of Yogini	19. Will reach a high status in yoga.

CHAPTER FOURTEEN

CONCLUSION

This book which started originally with the idea of providing a small post-graduate like thesis got expanded into the present full-length book.

From the scheme of the book it can be seen that while a safe and sound prediction can be given by applying the Yogini dasha, we have taken sufficient precaution to cross-check the predictions by employing the Vimshottari dasha also.

Not satisfied with this, we expanded the sphere of our research by bringing in the use of divisional horoscopes. We were confident that our use of the divisional horoscopes would add pointedness to scientific methodology of predictions adopted by us.

Over the years, it can be said with utmost satisfaction that Yogini dasha when employed along with Vimshottari dasha has given us remarkably accurate results. Yogini dasha is an important adjuvant to Vimshottari dasha and sheds light on certain areas which may not be clear on the application of Vimshottari dasha only. Yogini dasha applied as an additional dasha is also a confirmatory tool which makes the astrologer more confident about his predictions.

It must be remembered that we are engaged in astrology for a technological and industrial society and not for the ancient agricultural societies, for whom the fundamental principles of predictive astrology were formulated in those times. In the application and interpretation of the fundamental principles we have kept the modern society in view. It is for this reason that Sankata (Rahu) meaning trouble, can have brighter side to it also as we know that it is Rahu that shapes the career of engineers in our times. Similarly Ulka (Saturn) is not a negative period always as Saturn in our times is the giver of political power and technical education also on the positive side.

We had, however, taken the help of Mrs. Ratnam Neelkantan, a Sanskrit scholar, to give the classical meanings of the Yoginis which can give illuminating ideas for further research in Yogini dasha in future.

There are many other uses of Yogini dasha in which some progression is done by traditional astrologers which has been kept a secret so far. Since our aim is to give to our research, scientific methodology and replicability, we can only assure the readers that we welcome all useful suggestions and would endeavour to include them in the future editions of this book.

INDEX